Exploring England's Heritage

CUMBRIA TO NORTHUMBERLAND

John Weaver

Published in association with

English ❖ Heritage

London: HMSO

John Weaver is an historian, formerly an Inspector of Ancient Monuments, and author of guidebooks to Richmond Castle, North Yorkshire, Beeston Castle, Cheshire, and Boscobel House, Shropshire.

Robert Bewley is Air Survey Officer of RCHME, and author of *Prehistoric and Romano–British Settlement in the Solway Plain, Cumbria.*

© John Weaver 1992
Except chapter 1 © Robert Bewley 1992
Applications for reproduction should be made to HMSO
First published 1992
ISBN 0 11 300029 4

British Library Cataloguing in Publication Data

A CIP catalogue record for this book is available from the British Library

Front cover: Durham Castle, Framwellgate Bridge and the River Wear. Detail from painting by Edward Hastings, *c.*1815. Photo: Jarrold Publishing. Reproduced by kind permission of the Master, University College, Durham.
Back cover: The steam yacht *Gondala* on Coniston Water. Photo: NT/MIKE WILLIAMS.
Frontispiece: Bamburgh Castle, Northumberland. Photo: BTA.

Exploring England's Heritage
Other volumes already published in the series:

DEVON AND CORNWALL
Andrew Saunders
ISBN 0 11 300025 1

DORSET TO GLOUCESTERSHIRE
Martin Robertson
ISBN 0 11 300028 6

LONDON
Elain Harwood and Andrew Saint
ISBN 0 11 300032 4

HMSO publications are available from:

HMSO Publications Centre
(Mail, fax and telephone orders only)
PO Box 276, London SW8 5DT
Telephone orders 071-873 9090
General enquiries 071-873 0011
(queuing system in operation for both numbers)
Fax orders 071-873 8200

HMSO Bookshops
49 High Holborn, London WC1V 6HB
(counter service only)
071-873 0011   Fax 071-873 8200
258 Broad Street, Birmingham B1 2HE
021-643 3740   Fax 021-643 6510
Southey House, 33 Wine Street, Bristol BS1 2BQ
0272 264306   Fax 0272 294515
9–21 Princess Street, Manchester M60 8AS
061-834 7201   Fax 061-833 0634
16 Arthur Street, Belfast BT1 4GD
0232 238451   Fax 0232 235401
71 Lothian Road, Edinburgh EH3 9AZ
031-228 4181   Fax 031-229 2734

HMSO's Accredited Agents
(see Yellow Pages)

and through good booksellers

Printed in the UK for HMSO
Dd 294206   C80   8/92

Contents

Foreword

Today as midsummer approaches, Oxford is crammed with tourists. The roads near my office are choked with open-topped buses, their multilingual commentaries extolling the virtues of the city, while the pavements are impassable with crocodiles of visitors, eyes glued on the coloured umbrellas of determined guides. Dons wearing full academic dress attempt to make their way to and from the Examination Schools, to the delight of foreign photographers, and might as well be extras employed by the Tourist Board.

Oxford, Stratford-on-Avon and London together make up the golden triangle – golden, that is, to the tour operators – and millions of tourists are led through their crowded streets each year. The great majority of those who visit Oxford come for only a few hours, then move on to Stratford to stay overnight before returning to familiar London. It is London that takes the brunt. Westminster Abbey will be host to over 3 million, more than 2 million will visit the Tower of London, and then of course there are the museums and art galleries welcoming their annual tidal wave. Tourism, as governments are pleased to remind us, is one of Britain's biggest industries.

Looking at the tired, bewildered faces of the tourists off-loaded and scooped up again outside Oxford's St Giles, I long to grab them and say, 'It's all right – this is *not* what it's about. England is a beautiful, gentle country full of fascinating corners, breathtaking sights – an eclectic mix of insurpassable quality. All you need is someone with vision to show you how to start looking.'

Well, people with vision, as well as the knowledge of our cultural heritage and the ability to communicate, are not in ample supply, but the members of the team assembled to write the eleven volumes of *Exploring England's Heritage* share these qualities in abundance. Each author has a detailed and expert involvement, not only with the region they are writing about, but also with the buildings, the earthworks, the streets and the landscapes they have chosen to introduce us to. These guides are no mere compilations of well-worn facts, but original accounts coloured by the enthusiasm of people who know what makes a particular site so special.

Each volume introduces more than 100 places. Some are well known (who would dare to omit Stonehenge or Hadrian's Wall?); others are small-scale and obscure but no less interesting for that. We are led down alley-ways to admire hidden gems of architecture, into churchyards to search for inscribed stones and along canals to wonder at the skills of our early engineers. And of course there are the castles, the great houses and their gardens and the churches and cathedrals that give England its very particular character.

Exploring England's Heritage does not swamp you in facts. What each author does is to say, 'Let me show you something you might not have seen and tell you why I find it so particularly interesting.' What more could the discerning traveller want?

Barry Cunliffe

Acknowledgements

I am indebted to Robert Bewley for contributing the descriptions of prehistoric sites, and the introduction to that chapter. I am grateful also to Christopher Stell for his advice on Nonconformist chapels and to Geoffrey Trevelyan for many helpful comments. For information on individual sites I have been helped by Andrew Lowe (Duddon) and J W Almond (Ryhope), but to all owners, curators, and librarians who have kindly provided information I wish to record my thanks. I am grateful to Dawn Flower and Kate Morton for drawing the maps and plans, and to Barbara Gibson for transforming an untidy manuscript into an impeccable text. Stuart McLaren of HMSO has been a constant help, and the book owes much to his editorial skills.

In pursuit of illustrations my path has been eased by Anthony Kersting, Olive Cook (for Edwin Smith's photographs), and John Bethell, and by the staffs of the photographic libraries named below. Because they have borne the heaviest load I am indebted especially to the photographic librarians of English Heritage, the Royal Commission on the Historical Monuments of England, both in London and in Swindon, and of the University Committee for Aerial Photography in Cambridge.

Acknowledgements and thanks for permission to reproduce photographs are due to Aerofilms Ltd; John Bethel; Robert Bewley; Boys Syndication; British Academy; British Library; British Tourist Authority; Cambridge University Committee for Aerial Photography; J Allan Cash; Olive Cook; Country Life; Borough of Darlington Museum; Dean and Chapter of Durham Cathedral; Durham County Council Environmental Department; Durham University, Department of Archaeology; Master of University College, Durham University; T Gates; D W Harding; Historic Buildings and Monuments Commission; Tom Houghton; A F Kersting; T Middlemass; Ronald Mitchell; National Trust; Museum of Antiquities of the University and Society of Antiquities of Newcastle upon Tyne; North of England Open Air Museum, Beamish; Royal Commission on the Historical Monuments of England; Ryhope Engines Trust; Eddie Ryle-Hodges; Science Museum, London; Library of the Society of Friends; Barry Stacey/Lightwork; N E Stead; C F Stell; Tony Stone Worldwide; Sunderland Echo; Thomas Bewick Birthplace Trust; Colin R D Towers; Visionbank; Wetheriggs Country Pottery; and the Wordsworth Trust.

For permission to adapt site and town plans (gazetteer entries are given in bold) author and publisher are indebted to J Collingwood Bruce, *Handbook to the Roman Wall*, Newcastle, 1978 (**15**); B Hope-Taylor, *Yeavering*, HMSO, 1977 (**2**); S Johnson, *Hadrian's Wall*, English Heritage/Batsford, 1989 (for the map on page 16 and **16**); D Kear, 'Clifford's Fort and the Defence of the Tyne', *Archaeologia Aeliana*, 5th Series, vol. 14, the Society of Antiquaries of Newcastle upon Tyne, 1986 (**51**); Lake District National Park Authority (**100**); I MacIvor, *The Fortifications of Berwick-upon-Tweed*, English Heritage, 1989 (**49**); R Millward and A Robinson, *Cumbria*, Macmillan, 1972 (**61** and **64**); Ordnance Survey (**71**); W Rollinson, *Life and Tradition in the Lake District*, Dent, 1974 (**78**); Royal Archaeological Institute, *The Archaeological Journal*, vols 111, 115 and 133 (**66, 65** and **18** respectively); Royal Commission on the Historical Monuments of England, *Inventory of Westmorland*, HMSO, 1936 (**12**); and J T White, *The Scottish Border and Northumberland*, Methuen, 1973 (**76**).

Extracts from the following are reproduced by kind permission of the publisher: *First and Last Loves* by John Betjeman (John Murray); *The Buildings of England: Northumberland* (Penguin, 1957), © Nikolaus Pevsner, 1957; *The Buildings of England. County Durham* (Penguin, 1983), © Nikolaus Pevsner and Elizabeth Williamson, 1983; and *A History of the English Church and People* by Bede, (Penguin, 1965), © Leo Sherley-Price, 1955.

Notes for the Reader

Each site entry in *Exploring England's Heritage* is numbered and may be located easily on the end-map, but it is recommended especially for the more remote sites, that the visitor make use of the relevant Ordnance Survey map in the Landranger series. The location details of the site entries include a six-figure National Grid reference, e.g., NY 343337. Ordnance Survey maps show the National Grid and the following 1:50,000 maps will be found useful: 74, 75, 80, 81, 85, 86, 87, 88, 89, 90, 91, 92, 93, 96, 97, 98.

Readers should be aware that while the great majority of properties and sites referred to in this handbook are normally open to the public on a regular basis, others are open only on a limited basis. A few are not open at all, and may only be viewed from the public thoroughfare. In these circumstances readers are reminded to respect the owners' privacy. The *access codes* which appear at the end of each gazetteer entry are designed to indicate the level of public accessibility, and are explained below.

Access Codes

[A] site open for at least part of the year
[B] site open by appointment only
[C] site open by virtue of its use, e.g., road or church
[D] site not open but which may be seen from the public highway

Abbreviations

AFK   A F Kersting
C   Cumbria
CL   Country Life
CUCAP   Cambridge University Committee for Aerial Photography
D   County Durham
EH   English Heritage
N   Northumberland
NT   National Trust
OS   Ordnance Survey
RAI   Royal Archaeological Institute
RCHME   Royal Commission on the Historical Monuments of England
T   Tyne and Wear

Further Information

Further details on English Heritage, the Landmark Trust and the National Trust may be obtained from the following addresses:

English Heritage (Membership Dept), PO Box 1BB, London W1A 1BB

Landmark Trust, 21 Dean's Yard, Westminster, London SW1

National Trust (Membership Dept), PO Box 39, Bromley, Kent BR1 1NH

Introduction

Until 1974 the four northernmost English counties were Cumberland, Westmorland, Northumberland and County Durham, ancient and familiar names. Northumberland and County Durham still exist, although curtailed in size, but the new county of Cumbria now embraces both Cumberland and Westmorland, and, additionally, what was formerly Lancashire 'north of the sands'. Also new is the metropolitan county of Tyne and Wear, created from the urban centres of Newcastle, Gateshead and Sunderland, and their satellite towns.

Topographically the area divides into three main parts. On the west is the Lake District and its coastal fringes, with the Eden valley skirting its eastern flank and running north-west into the Solway plain. In the centre are the Pennines, merging, north of the Tyne, into the Northumberland hills and the Cheviots. On the east is a narrow coastal plain, bordering the North Sea, with enticing sands and rocky coves in its northern part, but with much industrial exploitation and spillage south of Ashington and along the Durham coast.

It is predominantly upland country. The mountains of the Lake District include the highest peaks in England, Scafell, Scafell Pike, Helvellyn, and Skiddaw, all more than 3,000ft (914 m). On the Pennine range, Cross Fell reaches 2,930ft (893 m), and on the Scottish border the summit of the Cheviot is 2,673ft (815 m).

The weather is often inclement, the rainfall in some localities high and the winds occasionally savage, but those who explore the area will find some of the most exhilarating landscapes in the British Isles and a remarkable variety of buildings and monuments.

Within the area are two National Parks. The Northumberland National Park covers 398 square miles (1,030 square km), from the Cheviot hills in the north to Hadrian's Wall in the south of the county. The Lake District National Park has within its 885 square miles (2,292 square km) most of the hill country west of the M6. Two major country walks cross its territory. The Pennine Way enters from the south at Tan Hill and heads north towards the Scottish border. Wainwright's Coast to Coast walk begins at St Bee's Head on the west coast and after threading through the Lake District leaves Cumbria at the head of Swaledale to make its way east to Robin Hood's Bay on the Yorkshire coast.

Parts of the area are heavily populated. The coalfields of Northumberland, County Durham and West Cumberland brought industry on an unprecedented scale, and workers in large numbers, into the region, and although coal and iron are no longer the mainsprings of the economy, the mining villages and industrial towns created by the Industrial Revolution still shape the character of the coalfield areas. However, by far the greater part of the region is thinly populated and rural. Its pattern of settlement is predominantly one of isolated farms, scattered hamlets, small villages and modest-sized market-towns. Its more typical buildings are those constructed by local craftsmen using materials gathered or quarried from near at hand. So in introducing the northern counties one should begin with rocks; they shape the landscape and determine the character of its buildings.

Rocks, Landscapes and Vernacular Buildings

The oldest rocks are to be found in the Lake District. The most ancient are the Skiddaw slates running in a band from Cockermouth to **Keswick** (69,C) and forming the huge, rounded mass of Skiddaw itself. Further south and slightly younger in the geological time-scale are the volcanic rocks of central Lakeland, whose spiky ridges and rocky

Head of Wasdale from Great Gable, Cumbria.
AFK

1

outcrops provide some of the most dramatic scenery in Britain and a choice of durable but intractable building stones, including, in a few places, granite. Pale pink and grey in colour, it occurs, and was used for building, in Eskdale, Ennerdale and at Threlkeld. From 1868 onwards it was quarried in large quantities at Shap (C), but almost entirely for use outside the area.

More widely used as a building material were 'cobbles', stones and boulders picked up from the fields and from beds of streams, and laid in their rough, untrimmed state in the walls of farmhouses and farm buildings, and in the drystone walls of the field boundaries. Even when covered with a coating of mortar and limewash the rugged character of the stonework is readily apparent and in the bare walls of barn, byre and field it is fully exposed.

Commonly used also were shales and slates. Shales provided rough blocks of hard dark stone. Lakeland slate, more easily riven, provided both material for walling and the trimmed and graded roofing slates whose variety of colours and textures are one of the joys of Lakeland buildings. They range from the olive green slates of **Honister** (101,C) to the blue and blue-grey slates of Furness (C) and south Lakeland. It is the traditional roof covering of the area. In the 17th century it was taken by packhorse and boat to London and the south, and was frequently used elsewhere.

Surrounding the central part of the Lake District are younger, softer rocks, mainly limestones and sandstones. To the south and south east a broad band of limestone forms the gentler hills of southern Lakeland and further east it shapes the open fells near Orton (C) and Kirkby Stephen (C), outcropping on the hillsides and appearing as limestone 'pavements' on the lower slopes. The stone varies from pale silvery grey to darker tones. It is prominent in the buildings of **Kendal** (68,C) and neighbouring towns, but in the countryside there is a tradition of plastering the stone walls of the farmhouses, and frequently of painting door jambs, windows and quoins in darker colours to give contrast and variety to otherwise sober facades.

Further north, along the Eden valley and around the coast from **Carlisle**

Stainmore, Cumbria. J ALLAN CASH

(65,C) to Ravenglass (C), sandstones predominate. The countryside is greener and milder, its fields hedged rather than walled, and the walls of its buildings showing shades of red and pink, brown and buff. The stone is easy to cut and shape so the walling is smooth and even, with the regularity of ashlar rather than rubble. It appears in the grander houses such as **Dalemain** (88,C), and in the smaller buildings of village and countryside.

East of the Eden valley are the Pennine hills of east Cumbria and County Durham. The tilt of the land and the general run of the rivers is eastwards with Tees, Wear, and Tyne emptying into the North Sea. Away from the valleys the countryside is harsh and bare, a solitary landscape of peat and heather moorland broken occasionally by isolated farms and the disused chimneys of abandoned lead-workings. The buildings are dark and sombre, built of millstone-grit whose coarse sandstones and shales form the topmost strata. Underneath are beds of limestone, outcropping on the west where the hills overlook the Eden and exposed in the lower slopes of the eastern valleys, where it was quarried for building and used extensively in recent times for industry and agriculture. At Frosterley in Weardale (D) an unusually hard limestone capable of taking a high polish was quarried in the later Middles Ages and employed in Durham churches, including Durham Cathedral, for paving and columns. It was used also in the great hall, now the chapel, of the bishop's palace at **Bishop Auckland** (32,D). A similar 'marble' was quarried at Dent (C), further to the west, and made into chimney pieces and other decorative items in the 18th and 19th centuries.

In Northumberland, the oldest rocks are those of the Cheviot Hills; volcanic in origin but smoothed by ice and general weathering into rounded shapes. Volcanic also are the coarse, crystalline rocks of the Whin Sill. Hard and jagged, they stand exposed at **Bamburgh** and **Dunstanburgh** (48 and 52,N) on the coast, and travel inland in ridges and escarpments. One of the ridges underpins a length of Hadrian's Wall and

Farmhouse near Dufton, Cumbria. BARRY STACEY/LIGHTWORK

outcrops in the rugged crags above Crag Lough. Other bands form the spectacular waterfalls at High Force on the River Tees, and shape the great natural amphitheatre of High Cup Nick (C) in the western Pennines. However, the building stone of Northumberland is pre-eminently sandstone. It was quarried locally by the Romans for the facing of Hadrian's Wall, and for their forts and living quarters. It was used by the builders of medieval castles and churches, and cut and laid with great precision in the walls of Georgian mansions. It can be honey-coloured, as at **Wallington** (96,N) and **Belsay** (86,N), or darker in tone, as at **Seaton Delaval** (94,N). In **Newcastle** (71,T) it can be seen in the medieval castle and town walls, and in the terraces, market halls, theatre, and railway station of the new town created by Grainger, Dobson and Clayton. It was used on roofs as well as in walls and has given the county an enviable and enduring quality of building.

There were, of course, other building materials used within the region. On the fringes of the Solway, clay-walled buildings with thatched roofs were once common, although few now survive. There were also buildings of timber. The great halls of the Anglian kings at **Yeavering** (31,N) were built of wood, and

the Normans used timber in their earliest castles (53,N) for palisades as well as for buildings. In the Middle Ages the hovels of the poor were probably at least partly of wood, and Surtees House in Newcastle and the Guildhall in Carlisle are reminders of a once extensive timber-framed tradition.

Brick before 1800 was rare. In Newcastle the Holy Jesus Hospital was built of brick in 1681, but in the 18th century it was used sparingly and mainly on the east coast. After 1800 it became the staple building material of cheap housing and part of the common vocabulary. However, even today stone has not lost its hold, although, regrettably, it is often at the expense of redundant barns and field houses demolished to provide facing stones for use elsewhere.

Settlement and Industry

Settlement in parts of the northern counties spans a period of more than 6,000 years, and industry has almost as long a sequence, if the Neolithic axe 'factory' of Langdale (C) in the Lake District may be so described. The most dramatic prehistoric remains in the North, as elsewhere, are those concerned with death, ritual and war. There are few sites more impressive than

3

The Cheviot Hills, Northumberland. AFK

the stone circles of **Castlerigg** (2,C) and Little Salkeld (7,C), or the great hillforts of **Carrock Fell** (1,C) **Humbleton Hill** and **Yeavering Bell** (5 and 10,N).

By comparison the traces of settlement are slight and elusive, but where the hill slopes and valley sides have escaped later cultivation the evidence of prehistoric settlement still survives, revealing the hut platforms of prehistoric villages as well as their field boundaries. In later prehistoric times settlements protected themselves with timber palisades, and in the last five centuries BC the massive defences of hillforts were built to shelter the communities within. However, even before the Roman conquest there was a movement to lower slopes, with huts and stockyards, such as those at **Burwens** (12,C) and on **Haystack Hill** (18,N) clustering together within a surrounding wall.

These native farms continued under Roman rule, supplying the conquerors with cattle and, to a lesser extent, grain, and underpinning with goods and labour the military economy of the North. They are dwarfed by the great military monuments of the Roman period. First and foremost is Hadrian's Wall, crossing the country from Wallsend (N) to Bowness-on-Solway (C) and extending south-westwards in an integrated but different form along the Cumbrian coast. It is not just a stone wall, as any visitor quickly appreciates, but a complex frontier system with forts for its troops, outposts to the north (23,C) and supporting bases to the south, all linked by roads and a cross-country communication system. Parts of the Wall have been robbed and others built over, but in the central section, from Sewingshields (N) to Walltown Crag (N), substantial remains of wall, turrets,

milecastles, earthworks and forts survive. One can walk along one of the greatest monuments of the Roman empire and enjoy also a superb landscape.

Roman industry was small-scale and mainly for local markets. Iron ore was mined and smelted in Northumberland for military uses, and other metals exploited, especially lead and silver. It was, under its military governors, a highly organised economy supported by an excellent road system, and it flourished for more than 300 years.

With the withdrawal of the Roman legions, the frontier collapsed and the northern area returned to tribalism. It was an age of minor kingdoms and petty kings and, on the east coast, of steadily increasing incursions by the English, first as warrior bands and then as colonists. The English kingdom of Bernicia was established during the 6th century with Bamburgh as one of its principal fortresses, and during the early years of the 7th century its kings extended their rule over the neighbouring kingdom of Deira to the south and over the Celtic kingdom of Rheged west of the Pennines. It became in its greater form the kingdom of Northumbria and, at the height of its power, stretched from the Forth to the Humber and across the country from the east coast to the west.

The site that tells us most about this period is Yeavering, where excavation revealed the halls and chambers of a royal palace. Nothing remains above ground, nor anything of the Celtic monastery on **Lindisfarne** (38,N), founded by Aidan in 635 at the invitation of King Oswald, but at **Monkwearmouth** (29,T), **Jarrow** (28,T), and **Escomb** (25,D), buildings survive that bring vividly to mind the age of Bede and the re-establishment of Christianity in northern England during the 7th century. Other reminders of the period of conversion are the standing crosses of the northern counties and especially those at **Bewcastle** (23,C) and at Ruthwell, now in Scotland but part of the territory of Northumbria in the 7th century.

Vikings sacked Lindisfarne in 793, Jarrow in 794 and **Tynemouth** (59,T) in 800. They ravaged the east coast, attacked and dismembered Northumbria, and in the 10th century established themselves in Cumbria. Their presence is recorded by a scatter of Scandinavian place names, and by sculptured crosses and tombstones with distinctive carvings of which the most striking are those at **Gosforth** (26,C) on the west coast.

In 954 Eric Bloodaxe, the last of the Scandinavian kings of York, was killed on Stainmore and Northumbria came under the control of Saxon kings. Its people were an amalgam of Britons, English, Danes and Norwegians, coexisting but divided by language and by culture. To the north was the kingdom of the Scots whose boundary on the east was the River Tweed, but on the west came south as far as Stainmore.

This was the northern inheritance of William I and his Norman lords who

seized the English throne in 1066, quelled resistance in the North and in 1072 forced the Scottish king to pay homage. They built castles to establish their control, many of them of earth and timber like **Elsdon** (53,N), whose earthworks have survived unaltered. Others were rebuilt in stone to guard the frontier and maintain a permanent military presence in the king's northern lands. Pre-eminent was **Durham** (66,D), the stronghold of the prince-bishop who ruled in the king's name and whose castle at **Norham** (57,N) was in the first line of border defence. On the west was the castle of Carlisle, built by William II to control the western routes from Scotland.

Until 1296 the pattern of life in the northern counties imitated that of the midlands and the south. The population increased and became more prosperous. However, in 1296 Edward I invaded Scotland and for the next 400 years the border counties were open to attack and plunder. Existing manor houses, like **Aydon** (73,N), were fortified; priests took refuge in towers (77,N); monasteries were fortified (39,C); old castles were strengthened and new ones built (54, N). Newcastle, Carlisle and Durham were ringed with walls and, in the country, landowners lived in tower-houses, like miniature fortresses. The imprint of those years of war can still be seen on every side.

The need for defence continued in the more exposed parts of the Border into the 16th century. **Berwick** (49,N) was given its massive artillery fortifications in the middle of the century, and Tynemouth also was strengthened. Bastle houses (75,N) were still being built and occupied in remote and exposed areas into the early years of the 17th century, but away from the more vulnerable parts there were signs of recovery. Farming and trade revived, and in the Lake District the first large-scale industry was started by immigrant German miners employed by the Company of Mines Royal (69,C). However, it was not until well into the 17th century that landowners felt sufficiently secure to add more comfortable wings to their medieval towers (86,N) and not until the later

years of the century that the 'great rebuilding', in progress 100 years earlier in the South, took place in the towns and countryside of the North.

Between 1650 and 1850 a vast amount of new building took place, catching up in part on the centuries frozen by war, but sponsored also by huge advances in agriculture and industry. The datestones on farmhouses testify to the widespread rebuilding of rural properties, first in Cumbria and on the Pennines and, following enclosure, on the larger estates of Northumberland. Villages and market-towns were transformed, replacing timber buildings with stone, and in the countryside Georgian mansions from **Rokeby Park** (93,D) to **Belsay** (86,N) brought elegance and luxury to the northern scene. Castles were not deserted but enlarged and improved and at **Alnwick** (47,N) and **Raby** (58,D) given interiors of renaissance splendour.

During the 18th century industry was well established in parts of the region, harnessing the plentiful supplies of water to drive its machinery. In the Lake District blast-furnaces, using local charcoal and water-powered bellows, were producing iron in rural locations (100,C), and woollen, flax, and bobbin mills (105,C) were also to be found near streams and rivers. In the Pennines lead-mining in the higher parts of the dales changed from a hand-operated industry to one using power-driven stamps and rollers for the crushing of ore (102,D), increasing output and establishing new communities in the area to provide an adequate labour force.

However, the key to the region's industrial progress in the last 200 years was coal. It fuelled the iron works of Workington (C), Millom (C) and Consett (D). Its transport forced the development of wagonways, railways and the steam locomotive. It promoted ship-building and engineering, and was an essential ingredient of the once extensive chemical industries on Tyneside. Colliery villages sprang up to house miners and their families, and the industrial towns grew hugely from trade and manufacturing. Suddenly most of the heavy industry has gone, and the region faces a different future.

Prehistoric Sites

by Robert Bewley

Factors influencing the nature of life and settlement in prehistoric times were all played out in a constantly changing climate. If one couples this fluid situation with the factors which have affected the discovery of archaeological sites, such as differential rates of destruction by natural and man-made agencies, the opportunities for understanding the nature of prehistoric settlement are limited.

These limitations are made worse in the four northernmost counties of England by the relatively small amount of archaeological survey which has been carried out in the area. If we look at extensive examination, such as aerial survey, we find that parts have been reasonably covered (the Solway Plain in Cumbria and the Millfield Basin in Northumberland for example). However, there is still a need for more systematic inspection. On the ground, some areas have been looked at in great detail (an area around Ingram Valley in the Cheviots by RCHME for example), and fieldwork by local archaeologists is transforming our understanding of the nature of settlement in the North. For example, fieldwork and excavation has proved the existence of a thriving Mesolithic population in the coastal area to the south of St Bees and Seascale in Cumbria.

There have also been excavations in County Durham which have begun to unearth the nature of prehistoric settlement in Teesdale and Weardale. In the Lake District National Park some of the uplands have been surveyed, recording cairn fields and settlements, but in no way can any of these provide all the answers to the questions we have about prehistoric settlements. They are a beginning and, hopefully, in another decade much more will be known. However, as this chapter shows the region contains a rich diversity of prehistoric archaeology.

The history (or prehistory) of settlement in the North really begins with the Mesolithic period (*c*.8000–4000 BC), although there are one or two Palaeolithic cave sites in the area (Kirkhead Cave in Cumbria for example). It is in the Neolithic period (*c*.4000–2000 BC), however, that the region was more densely settled and for which remains survive. There is more evidence for burial and ritual sites (henges and stone circles) and much less for the settlement aspects. This is partly due to the nature of Neolithic settlement, which has left little trace, but also because the research needed to understand and discover Neolithic settlement patterns in the area has only just begun.

The well-known Neolithic axe factory in Langdale (C) is an indication that the Lake District (as well as other areas) was occupied and used over 5,000 years ago. The 'ritual' henge monuments of **Mayburgh** (9,C) and **King Arthur's Round Table** (6,C) are, perhaps, connected to the stone-axe trade in some way and may be thought of as meeting-places, a cross between a cathedral and a supermarket.

For the Bronze Age (*c*.2000–800 BC), a similar story holds true and the archaeology of this period is one more of death than life. This is not to say that the region is without its Bronze Age monuments and examples such as the **Castlerigg Stone Circle** (2,C) are as evocative of prehistory as anywhere in the British Isles. In contrast the stone-built hillforts of Northumberland are a reminder of the times when protected settlements were necessary.

The Iron Age (*c*.800 BC–AD 50) is perhaps the most enigmatic of all the classic ages; there seems to be a north-east/north-west divide with a plethora of Iron Age farmsteads in the north-east but a distinct lack of similarly dated sites in the north-west. In Northumberland the palisaded settlements, especially the one described here, **High Knowes** (4,N),

Castlerigg Stone Circle. EH

Carrock Fell hillfort. R BEWLEY

is thought to be of Iron Age date.

The sites described here represent a very small sample of the total types and number. The intrepid explorer can discover much more information from the OS Landranger maps, as well as by contacting archaeological societies, the county archaeological officers or the National Archaeological Record at the RCHME, Fortress House, 23 Savile Row, London, W1X 2JQ.

1

Carrock Fell Hillfort, Cumbria
Bronze Age–Iron Age

OS 90 NY 343337. Mosedale. Reached via Mungrisdale, signposted off A66 Keswick to Penrith road. Carrock Fell is 1 mile (1.6km) NW of Mosedale along unfenced road, then by foot to site

[A]

Throughout the British Isles there are numerous hillforts, originally built from stone and timber with earthen ramparts. Cumbria, for some as yet unexplained reason, has very few but this is one of the most strikingly situated sites in the country at over 2,000ft (610 m) above mean sea level. The very steep climb up the eastern face of Carrock Fell is worth the considerable effort, especially on a clear day. The hillfort sits atop the eastern cliff-edge of the Skiddaw massif and commands a wide panorama to the north and west.

The fort has a stone rampart or wall enclosing about 5 acres (2ha) including a much denuded cairn. The enclosing wall is of drystone construction with possible entrances at the west end and along the southern side. Other gaps are visible and may be evidence of 'slighting' that is to say of deliberate destruction to make the defences unusable, but no excavations and very few surveys have been undertaken, so our knowledge of this fort and the era to which it belongs is very meagre. Hillforts are generally associated with the Iron Age (from *c.*800 BC to the arrival of the Romans in the

Cockfield Fell. D W HARDING

first century AD), but many have Bronze Age origins. The lack of any other Iron Age sites in the area may point to it having earlier beginnings as there is good evidence for a thriving Bronze Age community in Cumbria.

2

Castlerigg Stone Circle, Cumbria
Neolithic–Bronze Age

OS 90 NY 293236. Signposted off A66 Keswick–Penrith road, 1½ miles (2.4km) E of Keswick

[A] EH, NT

It has been said of Castlerigg that it is the most beautifully situated stone circle in England. There is no doubt it is an inspiring site to visit, especially in early morning or late evening.

The stone circle, measuring about a third of an acre, is also believed to be one of the earliest in England, having been constructed c.3000 BC. It has a flattened-circle shape, with a gap of nearly 11½ft (3.5 m) on the north side flanked by two massive stones, which may suggest an entrance. Within the site there is rectangle of ten stones, which is an unusual feature but of unknown function; there is also a very slight mound, perhaps a round barrow: the common form for burials in the Neolithic and Bronze Ages.

There have been no excavations here, but discoveries of Neolithic stone axes have been made within the site, suggesting early Neolithic activity. Speculation abounds as to the purposes of stone circles and they are often referred to as astronomical observatories. Castlerigg, like so many stone circles, can be used for observing solar and lunar alignments (of sunsets

and moonrises at different times of the year), but this does not prove they were used for this purpose in prehistoric times.

3

Cockfield Fell, County Durham
Iron Age–Romano-British and later

OS 92 NZ 120250. Cockfield. Signposted off A688 between Barnard Castle and Bishop Auckland. Site is N of Cockfield village on open common land

[A]

Although only the earliest earthwork features on Cockfield Fell are relevant to this section, the palimpsest nature of this unique landscape cannot fail to be of interest to all visitors. There are three groups of earthworks: prehistoric or Roman, medieval, and finally those relating to more recent industrial activities.

The three main prehistoric features are enclosures of varying sizes between 2.22 and 0.74 acres (0.9–0.3ha). They were probably settlements but are not defended in any way. The largest is an oval enclosure with two ramparts and a ditch in between the ramparts. It is crossed by a late 19th-century tramway and has been damaged by at least two drift mines. The other two enclosures are roughly rectangular, and the smallest one could well be a late Iron Age native farmstead.

It is a remarkable coincidence of events which has allowed the earthworks on Cockfield Fell to remain visible in a island of unimproved pasture. By the end of the Industrial Revolution the area was in decline and was probably not suitable for agricultural improvement. Then in 1868 the freeholders of the Fell were allotted grazing rights, divided into 1,100 'stints' which specified the number of animals allowed on the land. Thus the land was maintained as pasture and is still managed today by the Field Reeves, many of whom live in the houses on the Fell.

High Knowes. RCHME

4

High Knowes, Northumberland
Iron Age–Romano-British

OS 81 NT 970124 (site A) and NT 972125 (site B). Alnham (NT 995109). Reached by minor roads off A697 or B6341. From the village take narrow road towards Ewartly Shank farm. Sites are below summit of hill

[A]

There are two settlements at High Knowes, referred to as A and B. The sites are usually described as 'palisaded homesteads' and at A the outer enclosing circle of about 150ft (45.72 m) in diameter has a palisade trench with a second one 10ft (3.04 m) inside. Within the 'homestead' there are four circular wooden-built houses, one of which was fully excavated in 1962 and 1963. No artefacts were found during the excavation, nor any charcoal for radiocarbon dating.

At the adjacent site (B), the settlement is pear-shaped and is defined by two palisade trenches 5ft (1.52 m) apart. Although this site is only just over half an acre in area it contains the remains of some sixteen timber-built houses. The remains of a stone-built hut, which appeared to overlie the entrance, were excavated in 1962. The stone work is reminiscent of Romano-British workmanship and the coarse pottery also suggests that the stone hut was overlying an Iron Age site. This supports the view that these are Iron Age settlements which were re-used at a later date during the Roman occupation.

5

Humbleton Hill Hillfort, Northumberland
Bronze Age–Iron Age

OS 74 and 75 NT 966282. Humbleton. 1 mile (1.6km) NW of Wooler off A697

[A]

It is possible to approach this hillfort via a steep climb up the south-east slope of Humbleton Hill. A longer and only slightly less strenuous route is up the footpaths which skirt the bottom of the hill to the north and gradually rise to the summit from the west. Whichever route is chosen the effort will be rewarded by the sight of the massive stone ramparts of the hillfort, so wide in parts that local shepherds have made sheepfolds within the walls.

The hillfort itself is the inner enclosure, with two outer encircling enclosures. The largest of these annexes takes in the lower, flatter ground to the west, whilst the hillfort and its immediate annexe occupy the summit of the hill. The size and shape of the site suggest that the fort began life in the Bronze Age as a single enclosure which was then added to during the Iron Age, and possibly continued into the Romano-British period. The hillfort has been described as a 'citadel' type as it stands on a commanding hill-top overlooking the Millfield Basin.

Humbleton Hill hillfort. RCHME

showed that large monoliths once stood on either side of the entrance. A connection with Mayburgh (9,C) is suggested by the entrance of Mayburgh leading directly towards this henge, but the nature of this connection has yet to be proved.

7

Long Meg and her Daughters, Cumbria
Neolithic–Bronze Age

OS 91 NY 571372. Little Salkeld. Leave A686 Penrith–Alston road at Langwathby. Site is ¾ miles (1.2 km) N of Little Salkeld village
[A] EH

Long Meg is one of the largest stone circles in Britain after Avebury in Wiltshire and Stanton Drew in Avon, measuring 357ft by 305ft (109 m by 93 m). As you approach the site Long Meg herself, a single standing stone 12ft (3.7 m) in height stands apart from her Daughters (the stones of the circle). There are a number of incised carvings (circles and spirals) on the sides of this tall obelisk, a type of decoration usually associated with Bronze Age artwork (c.2000–900 BC).

Legend has it that Long Meg and her Daughters were a coven of witches turned to stone by a magician as they celebrated their sabbath. More scientific research, through aerial photography, has revealed a curvilinear ditched enclosure of over 10 acres (4.18ha) to the north of the stone circle in which some of the stones have been placed, or even slipped. This suggests near contemporaneity of the stone circle and the ditch. Further research may provide a better date for the site than the suggested late Neolithic–early Bronze Age one of c.2500–2000 BC.

Those who have studied the astronomical alignment at Long Meg say that if you sit in the centre of the circle you can watch the winter sun set behind Long Meg herself. The presence of 'outlying' stones around stone circles adds weight to the argument that they

King Arthur's Round Table (bottom left) and Mayburgh henge (top right). R BEWLEY

6

King Arthur's Round Table, Cumbria
Neolithic–Bronze Age

OS 90 NY 523284. Eamont Bridge. 1 mile (1.6km) S of Penrith by A66, then onto B5320. EH signposted
[A] EH

This once impressive henge, a little under 54 yards (c.45 m) in diameter, has been clipped by two roads and has had its centre artificially raised by the landlord of the local pub (in 1820) for use as a tea-garden. Despite this, and a series of excavations in 1937 and 1939, the site survives as an impressive earthwork monument. The excavations found no sign of a former stone circle within the henge nor any datable artefacts. The original north-west entrance was destroyed by the construction and widening of the roads and an early sketch, in the 17th century, were used in some way for measuring the length of seasons through the position of the sun and moon.

8

Lordenshaws, Northumberland
Bronze Age–Romano-British

OS 81 NZ 054993. 3 miles (4.8km) S of Rothbury on B6342, then turn off to Lordenshaw

[A]

The hillfort covers a moorland spur 800ft (243.84 m) above sea level. It has three ramparts and ditches as well as a counterscarp bank; the defences are about 120ft (36.57 m) wide overall. The inner bank rises to a maximum height of just over 6½ft (2 m) in places and encloses about three quarters of an acre (0.3ha). The main entrances are to the east and west. Inside, like a number of hillforts in Northumberland, there is evidence of Romano-British hut circles, some of which overlie the south-eastern defences.

Within the immediate vicinity of the hillfort are two stones with cup and ring marks, as well as six cairns, including a stone cist to the north-east of the fort itself. To the south-west of the fort there is an earthwork dyke, 30ft wide and 4ft high (9.1 by 1.2 m) which seems to have extended across the hill between the two valleys. The fort itself is thought to be Iron Age in origin, but has obviously been added to in later periods, especially in the Romano-British period, and perhaps even into medieval times.

9

Mayburgh, Cumbria
Neolithic–Bronze Age

OS 90 NY 519285. Eamont Bridge. 1 mile (1.6km) S of Penrith by A66, then B5320. EH signposted

[A] EH

The junction of two rivers, the Eamont and the Lowther, has given rise to the siting of two very impressive henge

Long Meg and Her Daughters. COLIN R D TOWERS

Lordenshaws hillfort. T GATES

monuments. The stone ramparts of Mayburgh henge are only a few hundred yards from the earth bank and ditch of King Arthur's Round Table henge (6,C). Mayburgh's stone bank, about 95 yards (87 m) in diameter, encloses about 1½ acres (0.6ha) and is constructed of river boulders to a maximum height of over 12ft (3.6 m). The construction of this very large bank is visible today as a number of the trees which had taken root on the bank have been blown down, revealing the large boulders.

The single standing stone in the centre of the henge is all that remains of one or perhaps two inner stone circles. The original entrance is to the east side, although there is a modern gap on the south-west. Surveys have revealed an internal quarry ditch. No excavations have taken place here, but chance discoveries of Neolithic stone axes as well as a bronze axe suggest a Neolithic to Bronze Age date.

The function of henges is a central question in prehistoric archaeology and the position of Mayburgh at the confluence of two rivers has given rise to the suggestions that it was a re-distribution centre along a Neolithic stone axe trade route, the Neolithic axe factory at Langdale, (C) being the probable source of the stone axes.

10

Yeavering Bell Hillfort, Northumberland
Bronze Age–Iron Age

OS 74 and 75 NT 928293. Wooler. A697 then B6351 from Wooler to Yeavering Bell farm, then by foot, or, if time available, along footpaths from Wooler

[A]

The whole area around Yeavering Bell, which overlooks the rivers Glen and Till, has had a long history of occupation: from Neolithic henges through to Iron Age settlements and culminating in the royal palace of Adgefrin, just west of the farm at Old Yeavering (31,N).

The hillfort on Yeavering Bell is the largest in Northumberland, covering some 15 acres (6ha) and has been likened to an *oppidum* (small town) on account of the 130 or so hut circles within the stone walls. The enclosing stone walls girdle the summit of the Bell and take in a large mound or cairn on the eastern end of the summit. This mound is partly natural and partly artificial and is itself surrounded by a palisade trench. The palisade encloses an area of more level ground to the south-west of the mound; its purpose is yet unknown.

The main entrance to the fort is to the south, although there is evidence for entrances on all four cardinal points. The southern entrance has faint traces of something which may have been a guardroom. If one leaves the fort by the southern entrance the slopes there are terraced, perhaps indicative of agricultural practices very near to the fort and at a higher altitude than would be possible today. Grazing is about the limit nowadays, and there is a herd of feral goats which roam these moors.

Excavations in the 19th century revealed that the walls of the fort are 10–12ft (3–3.6 m) thick and probably stood 7–8ft (2.1–2.4 m) high. A number of the hut circles, or platforms, which are visible within the fort, were also excavated providing pottery, flint and jasper: all indications of dwelling places. The fort is usually thought to be of Iron Age date (though it may have had earlier origins) with later, Romano-British occupation.

Yeavering Bell hillfort. CUCAP

13

Hadrian's Wall. EH

Sestertius of Hadrian. UNIVERSITY OF
NEWCASTLE UPON TYNE, MUSEUM OF ANTIQUITIES

Romano-British Sites

The outstanding monument of the Roman period in Britain is Hadrian's Wall, not just a wall but a complex defensive system designed, according to Hadrian's biographer, to 'separate the Romans from the Barbarians.' It was built, ultimately, from Wallsend on the east to Bowness-on-Solway on the west, following the valleys of the Tyne and the Irthing, but taking the high ground on the northern side to obtain the best defensive positions. Its length is 80 Roman miles or approximately 73 English miles (117km).

The building of the defences began shortly after AD 122 on the orders of the emperor Hadrian, after attacks by hostile tribesmen on Roman garrisons further north. It was planned as a stone wall 10 (Roman) feet wide as far as the River Irthing, then as a turf wall from the Irthing westwards, but later modifications resulted in a slightly narrower wall for much of its length and the use of stone as building material throughout. Its height is not known. Its maximum surviving height, which occurs but rarely, is 11ft (3.3 m), but it may have reached 15ft (4.9 m) in places.

It was not intended to be a passive barrier, nor to seal the frontier completely. Spaced a mile apart were small forts, known as milecastles, and between them, at every third of a mile, turrets or watch-towers whose purpose was to give warning of hostile tribesmen. The main body of troops was concentrated in forts such as **Housesteads** (20,N) and **Birdoswald** (11,C), permanent bases capable of housing up to 1,000 men. These were the fighting garrisons ready to quell uprisings whether to the north or to the south. The earliest forts were slightly to the south of the stone wall, but later modifications established forts on the line of the wall itself.

On the north side of the stone wall was a ditch, usually about 27ft (8.23 m) wide, except where cliffs or other natural barriers made it unnecessary, and to the south, at varying distances from the wall

ran the *vallum*, another ditch with banks on either side, sealing off, like a barbed-wire barricade, a prohibited zone on the south side of the wall.

Further to the north were outpost forts, for example at High Rochester (N) and Bewcastle (23,C), and to the rear were supply stations such as those at Corbridge (N) and South Shields (T) handling supplies brought in by sea and transported inland. Serving the garrisons and maintaining communications was a network of roads which extended south to the military headquarters at York. The principal routes were from Corbridge through forts at Ebchester (D), Lanchester (D) and Binchester (D); and, on the western side of the Pennines from Carlisle (65,C) south to the fort at Brougham (50,C), then south-east via Brough (64,C) and Bowes (D) to join the Corbridge to York road near Catterick in North Yorkshire.

To guard the vulnerable west coast, a system of small forts and towers, similar to the milecastles and turrets of the Wall itself, but without the connecting masonry, extended along the edge of the coastal area for a distance of 26 miles (41.8km) to give further protection against the northern tribes (16,C). Within the mountains of the north-west, forts were established at strategic sites like **Hardknott** (17,C) and Ambleside (C), with connecting roads, to ensure that the area remained in the grip of military control.

The frontier was maintained for nearly 300 years. At one time the Wall was abandoned in favour of a more northerly barrier, the Antonine Wall, across the Forth–Clyde isthmus, but for most of the period Hadrian's Wall was the northern frontier of Roman Britain, and its hinterland to the south, present-day Cumbria and County Durham, was held in military occupation. There were few towns and only one known Roman villa. Civilian settlements and markets developed outside the forts, providing goods and services for the garrisons, but they were small in size and tied firmly to

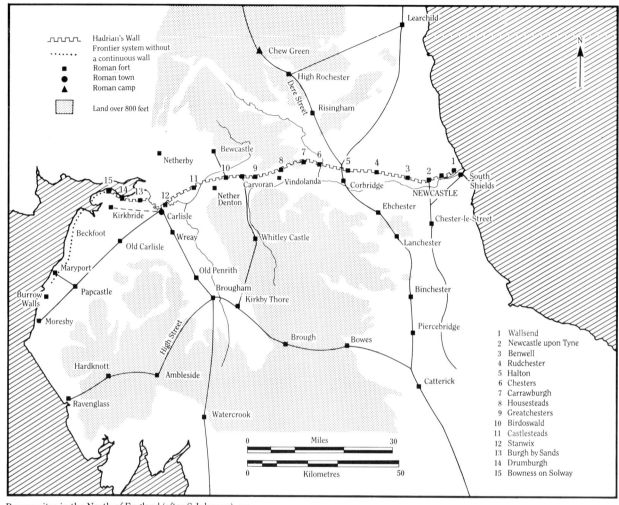

Roman sites in the North of England (after S Johnson). EH

the needs of the military. In the countryside native farms and settlements survived and continued in use, their inhabitants taxed and supervised and made to contribute to the Roman economy. Aerial photography, among other work, has revealed the extent of these settlements spreading not only over the higher lands, where their remains are readily visible (12,C and 18,N), but also along the valleys and coastal plains where later cultivation has destroyed all surface remains.

To appreciate the scale and extent of the Wall it is best to visit the central section and to examine it on foot, starting at Housesteads or, further west,

at Winshields or Walltown. The forts are easily accessible and those at Housesteads, Chesters and **Vindolanda** (21,N) have excellent museums, as do Corbridge (N) and South Shields (T). Wallsend, the eastern terminus, has a heritage centre with excavation finds and information near the laid-out remains, and there are very informative museums in Newcastle (University Museum of Antiquities) and Carlisle (Tullie House Museum).

Opinions may differ as to which site best captures the Roman achievement in the North, whether it is the lonely outpost at **Chew Green** (15,N), the fellside fort at Hardknott, the majestic roads (14 and 19,C), or some part of the

Wall itself. Few would dispute that, taken as a whole, it is an immensely impressive record of an imposed order whose imprint is still plainly visible even at this distance of time.

11

Birdoswald, Cumbria
Roman

OS 86 NY 615663. Gilsland. 1 mile (1.6km) W of Gilsland on B6318 and minor road

[A] EH, Cumbria County Council

The Roman fort at Birdoswald (Banna) is close to the River Irthing and probably one of its purposes was to protect the river crossing. It stands on high ground above the river and covers about 5 acres (3ha). Past excavations have recorded the plan of the principal buildings, but until acquisition by Cumbria County Council, the fort was part of a working farm and its interior was used as valuable cattle pasture. Little, therefore, remained on display except for substantial parts of the fort wall, the gates and interval towers. An exhibition centre and shop have now been installed in the farm buildings, and excavations have examined the fort's granaries, west gate and part of the north wall. It has been shown that the farmhouse, which is built round a 16th-century bastle, has medieval origins. Finds from the excavations are in Tullie House Museum, Carlisle.

A fine stretch of Roman wall, in which there are a number of centurial and other carved stones, runs from the north-east corner of the fort eastwards and includes a milecastle almost on the edge of the steep slope above the river. It is unwise to attempt any descent of this bank. To see the remains of the Roman bridge and another excellent length of wall with interval turrets it is necessary to return to the fort and travel by road or path to Gilsland village (N). Near the railway station in Gilsland village is another milecastle, on the slopes above Poltross Burn.

West of Birdoswald a minor road runs to Banks village (C) generally following the line of the Wall. Remains of wall turrets as well as lengths of ditch and *vallum* are to be found along the road and also traces of the turf wall, the predecessor of the stone wall in the area west of the River Irthing. The remains in this section of the Wall are not spectacular but they reveal, perhaps better than any other part, the early development of this great defensive work, and the story of their elucidation is well worth pursuing. At Pike Hill (C) are parts of a signal tower built at an angle of 45 degrees from the line of the Roman wall and thought to have been used for long distance signalling.

Birdoswald fort. EH

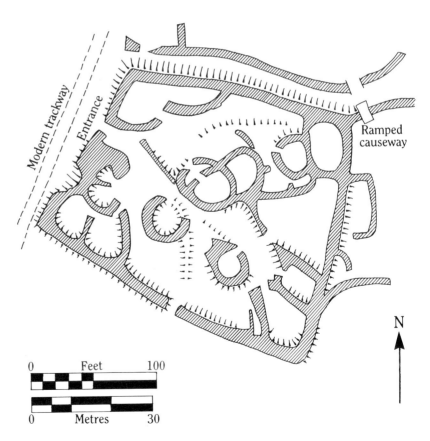

Burwens settlement (after RCHME). EH

12

Burwens Native Settlement, Cumbria
Pre-Roman (?), Roman and later

OS 91 NY 622123. N of Orton on B6260, then minor road. Site is N of Crosby Lodge

[D]

Burwens is one of a cluster of settlement sites on the limestone upland of Crosby Ravensworth Fell. It consists of a rectangular enclosure covering nearly one acre (0.4ha) which has within its walls several hut circles, some abutting the walls and others free-standing. The largest is about 25ft (7.5 m) in diameter. Between the huts are passages to small enclosed spaces which may have been cattle pens. To the north and east are the walls of an associated field system covering a further 3–4 acres (1.2–1.6ha).

Excavations at Ewe Close (no public access), about 1 mile (1.5km) to the north revealed a similar cluster of huts within a rectangular enclosure, and there are other groups nearby. The huts had stone walls up to 6ft (1.8 m) thick and two of those investigated had hearths. The conical roofs were probably covered with turf or thatch on wooden poles which rested on the walls. The Ewe Close settlement appears to be earlier than the Roman road which runs nearby and to have continued in use through the Roman period, and possibly beyond. Burwens may have had a similar history but its site has not been excavated.

Until recently the majority of known settlements of this date were on marginal land in the upland areas. Further work, especially aerial photography, has shown this to be only part of the pattern of rural settlement. The lower and more fertile areas were also settled and farmed, but continued use of the better agricultural land has left fewer visible remains on the ground.

13

Carrawburgh, Northumberland
Roman

OS 87 NY 859712. Chollerford. 4 miles (6.4km) W of Chollerford on B6318

[A] EH (temple)

The outline of Carrawburgh fort (Brocolitia) can be traced on the ground by its ramparts and ditch, but there has been very little excavation within the

Temple of Mithras, Carrawburgh. EH

fort and the only exposed masonry is the wall of the granary.

The Mithraeum is outside the fort and is reached by a footpath skirting its south-east corner. The temple was discovered in 1949 during a very dry summer and excavated the following year. It is rectangular in plan and measures 36ft by 15ft (9 m by 4.5 m), though in its original form it was smaller. Internally it is divided by a screen into two parts, a small ante-room, probably for those not yet initiated into the cult, and the larger main body of the temple. This had side benches on which worshippers knelt or reclined, with small altars in front of the benches, and statues of Cautes and Cautopates, attendants of the god, at the ends. At the far end is the sanctuary with three altars dedicated to Mithras by commanders of the fort. The left-hand altar is carved with a half-length representation of the god, pierced to allow light to shine through his crown. As the interior was dimly lit, simulating a cave, no doubt the effect was dramatic. Behind the altars, within a recess, was a carving of Mithras slaying the bull, symbolising the triumph of good over evil.

Mithraism was an ancient eastern religion adopted by the Romans and was popular in the army, especially among senior officers. There were temples at Rudchester (N) and Housesteads (20,N) and dedications have been found at Castlesteads (C) and High Rochester (N). The altars and sculptures in the Carrawburgh temple are replicas of the originals which are now in the University Museum of Antiquities in Newcastle, where there is a full-scale reconstruction of the Mithraeum.

Near the temple is a spring dedicated to the Celtic water goddess, Coventina. Objects found in the pool at the centre of the shrine, which does not survive, are in the museum at Chesters. The bath-house, known from excavation, was between the shrine and the fort, among the buildings of the *vicus* which spread over the slopes south and west of the fort.

The Roman wall at Carrawburgh is under the road and there is little to see of it until Sewingshields (N) on the west and Black Carts (N) on the east.

Travelling east towards Chesters both ditch and *vallum* are well preserved. Chesters fort (N) is 3.5 miles (5.6km) east of Carrawburgh. It is partly excavated, and displayed rather uncomfortably in small fenced compartments, but the bath-house is very well preserved. There is a site museum and a shop.

14

Catterick to Brougham Roman Road, North Yorkshire, County Durham and Cumbria
Roman and modern

OS 90–93 SE 215053 (Scotch Corner) to NY 537290 (Brougham). Follow route of A66 from North Yorkshire to Penrith

[C]

Despite modern changes, the A66 road across the northern Pennines still bears the stamp of Roman engineering and for much of its length follows the route of the Roman road. On the east, at Scotch Corner in North Yorkshire, it leaves the Roman road (Dere Street) which heads north towards Corbridge, and runs instead in a north-westerly direction passing a series of forts established along its route. At Greta Bridge (D) the Roman fort survives as an earthwork in the fields behind the Morritt Arms hotel. Further west is the fort at Bowes (D) now partly occupied by the medieval church and castle. At Rey Cross (D), the highest point of the road and summit of the Stainmore Pass, is a marching camp earlier than the road and possibly established by Petillius Cerialis, governor of Britain, during the conquest of Brigantia AD 71–4. The ramparts of the camp are clearly visible on both sides of the road. Also on high ground nearby, but less easily detectable, are the sites of Roman signal stations, part of a system linking the forts along the road and ensuring rapid communication across the country.

From the summit the road descends through Stainmore to Brough (64,C) where, again, a castle occupies part of

the Roman fort. It then moves westwards through gentler country to forts at Kirkby Thore (C) and Brougham (50,C), passing another marching camp at Crackenthorpe, near Appleby (C). At Kirkby Thore a secondary road branches north to Alston (C) and its associated lead mines. At Brougham the road meets the north–south route established by the Romans between Carlisle and Lancaster, and the Roman road heading south-west towards Ambleside, High Street (19,C). The fort at Brougham lies in the fields to the south of the castle.

This Pennine route is one of great antiquity, the easiest crossing from the Eden valley and Lake District to the eastern plains and coast, and in continuous use from prehistoric times onwards. Visually and historically, it is one of the most exciting roads in Britain, its strategic importance in the Roman period measured by its sequence of forts and other military posts, and echoed by the great medieval fortresses which also marks its route, often on the same sites. One should pause, too, at Rey Cross, if the thundering traffic of the modern highway allows, to consider that in the 11th century this marked the southern boundary of the kingdom of the Scots and, therefore, for a time this was truly a border road. A century earlier, in 954, on the slopes to the west, Eric Bloodaxe, last Scandinavian king of York, was slain on a waste place called 'Steinmor' while using this same route across the hills.

15

Chew Green Roman Camps, Northumberland
Roman

OS 80 NT 788085. Redesdale Forest. A68 to Redesdale Camp, then by track and path for about 6½ miles (10.5km). Alternatively, follow the Pennine Way from Byrness, a walk of about 4½ miles (7.2km) each way

[A]

Chew Green is not easily accessible. The site is remote and the weather often inclement, but it has been described by

19

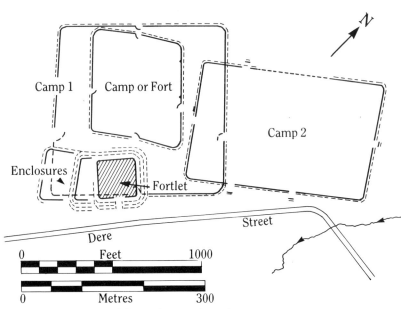

Chew Green Roman camps (after J Collingwood Bruce). EH

Ian Richmond in Pevsner's *Northumberland* as 'the most remarkable visible group of Roman earthworks in Britain.' Visitors should go appropriately equipped and obtain the necessary permission from the duty officer at Redesdale Camp if approaching through the military range.

The camps are close to the Roman road (Dere Street) heading north from Corbridge to Scotland and during its course negotiating the headwaters of the River Coquet. Four earthworks are visible. The two largest are marching camps, the most southerly of the two capable of accommodating a legion and probably belonging to Agricola's advance northwards *c*.AD 80. Associated with this is a small fortlet established by excavation but not visible on the ground.

Later in date and partially over-lapping the south camp is a second marching camp only slightly smaller than the first but on a different alignment to allow a third camp to be built within the first. The third earthwork has been interpreted as a camp accommodating those engaged on road making and bridge building in the area, but its substantial defences and

other features suggest that it may have been built as a fort for long-term use. The fourth earthwork is a small fortlet with a triple ditch which has attached to it on its south side two protected enclosures, possibly used as wagon parks for those travelling along the road and needing overnight security. Trial excavation has established that the fortlet was occupied well into the 2nd century but no evidence was found of later use. Pieces of burnt timber and of wattle and daub were found within the fortlet.

16

Coastal Defences, Cumbria
Roman

OS 85 and 89 NY 225628 (Bowness-on-Solway) to NY 025348 (Risehow). Follow Cumbrian coastline, B5307, B5302, B5300, A 596 and minor roads

[D]

The continuous defences of Hadrian's Wall ended on the west coast at the fort of Maia, now buried under the village of

Bowness-on-Solway (C). However, to guard the vulnerable coast south of Bowness, a chain of fortlets and towers was built along the coast for a distance of about 26 miles (41.8km). The fortlets, equivalent to the milecastles on the Wall itself, had turf ramparts and contained a timber barrack or barracks for a small garrison. The towers, about 20ft (6 m) square, were built of stone and each had an internal staircase to give access to a look-out platform on the top. They were regularly spaced with two towers between each pair of fortlets, and they were free-standing. Their remains consist of earthworks proved by excavation and, where nothing survives on the ground, of sites revealed by aerial photography.

The purpose of the system was to maintain a watch on coastal traffic and to give warning of raids from across the Solway Firth. Unlike the Wall there was no continuous barrier, but there was support near at hand from the garrisons of four forts along the coast at Beckfoot (Bibra), Maryport (Alauna), Burrow Walls, and Moresby (Gabrosentum), and from inland cavalry forts at Papcastle (Derventio) and Old Carlisle (Olenacum). It has been surmised that the system extended further along the coast as far as St Bee's Head, but the most southerly point that has been established with certainty is at Risehow near Flimby (C).

17

Hardknott Castle, Cumbria
Roman

OS 89 NY 218015. Eskdale. Site at W end of Hardknott Pass, 9 miles (14.5km) NE of Ravenglass

[A] EH

The modern road to the fort, whether one approaches from the east or from the west, is narrow, steep and full of bends. Drivers should exercise care and trailers are not recommended. Nevertheless those who negotiate it will be rewarded by the interest of the site and by the grandeur of the surrounding hills.

Despite its name this is the Roman fort of Mediobogdum, an early 2nd-century fort begun under Trajan and finished during the reign of Hadrian. It is sited at the head of Eskdale, on a spur of land under Hardknott Fell, controlling both the valley and the Roman road across the mountains from Ambleside (Galava) in the east to Ravenglass (Glannaventa) on the west coast.

The fort covers about 3 acres (1.2ha) and has a stone-fronted rampart, part of which has been rebuilt from fallen masonry. A slate course distinguishes the original masonry from the rebuilt stones. In each corner of the fort are the foundations of angle towers and there are gateways in all four sides, three with double portals but that on the north having only a single opening. The west gateway has a surviving pivot hole for one of its gates. Within the fort, the commandant's house, headquarters building, and a granary have been excavated and the surviving masonry preserved. The rest of the fort has yet to be examined.

Outside the fort is a bath-house, on the slope to the south-east, and to the east, higher up the hill, is a large parade ground for the training and exercise of the garrison. The ground has been levelled and embanked to form a useable area on the sloping ground, and on its west side is a ramp leading to a tribunal or viewing platform for the officer commanding the military exercises. Here in the hills is the best preserved Roman parade ground in the country.

18
Haystack Hill Native Settlement, Northumberland
Roman and later

OS 81 NU 006150. Ingram. Leave A697 S of Wooler at junction for Ingram. Site then reached by footpath at W end of village

[A]

The settlement is on the slopes of the hill and consists of four walled enclosures, three of them circular and the fourth approximately rectangular in plan, containing, altogether, about fifteen round huts. In the circular enclosures the huts are built fronting on to walled yards which have been interpreted as stockyards. The rectangular enclosure has a different internal arrangement and the remains of a rectangular building, and is possibly the result of later re-occupation.

Excavations on other sites have found hearths, areas of paving and the remains of benching inside the huts, and evidence of timber uprights to support the roofs. Dating evidence ranges from the early 2nd to 4th centuries AD, but occupation may have continued beyond the Roman period and, as on this site, there are indications of later re-use.

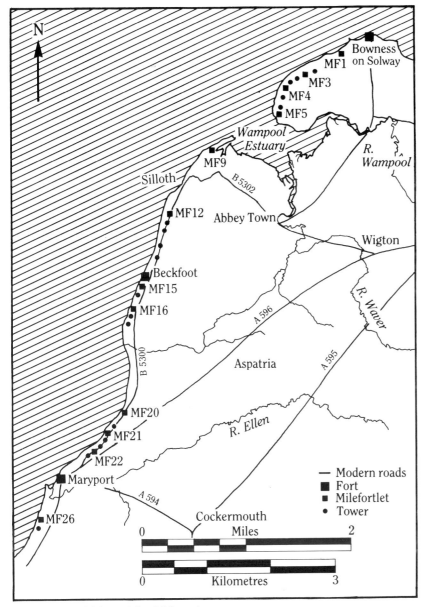

Cumbrian coastal defences (after S Johnson). EH

21

Hardknott fort. AEROFILMS

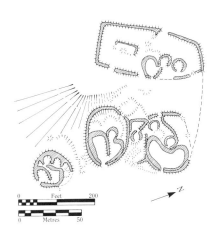

Haystack Hill (after RAI). EH

Romano-British settlements of this type survive in large numbers on the hill-slopes in the north of the county and across the border in south-east Scotland, but there is no reason to think they were limited to the higher ground. They may well have spread across other areas including the coastal plain, employing, in different parts, timber rather than stone. To the south, and immediately north of Hadrian's Wall,

there are similar walled enclosures with round huts, but the enclosures are straight-sided rather than circular. They are also more regularly spaced and follow a more uniform plan, arguing perhaps, a greater measure of administrative control.

19
High Street Roman Road, Cumbria
Roman

OS 90 NY 537290 (Brougham) to NY 421055 (Troutbeck Park). The route of the Roman road runs from Brougham, 1½ miles (2.4km) SE of Penrith on A66 to Troutbeck Park, 5 miles (8km) N of Windermere on A592

[A]

The Roman road known as High Street runs from the fort at Brougham (Brocavum) towards the fort at Ambleside (Galava), a distance of approximately 19 miles (31km). Its route at each end is still a matter of

debate, but the central section has been established by excavation and by surviving vestiges of the road and its ditches. Its course is described in a number of guides including Wainwright's *The Far Eastern Fells*, Kendal, 1959. It crosses open moorland and reaches heights of more than 2,000ft (610 m), passing close to High Street summit which is 2,718ft (828 m) above sea level. It can be walked, but the normal precautions and equipment for walking on the high fells are essential.

20
Housesteads Fort, Northumberland
Roman

OS 87 NY 790688. Bardon Mill. Site is 2¾ miles (4.4km) NE of Bardon Mill off B6318

[A] EH, NT

Housesteads fort (Vercovicium) is the most impressive of all the forts of Hadrian's Wall. Its outer walls stand to 10ft (3 m) in height and its principal buildings have been excavated and laid out so it is possible to see how the fort was organised. It also has a superb position commanding great sweeps of land to the north and south. It occupies about 5 acres (2ha) of ground on a high ridge, with a stream, the Knag Burn, in a small valley to the east.

At the heart of the fort is the headquarters building with an assembly hall at the end of a courtyard and, behind the hall, the regimental chapel and administrative offices. The commandant's house is to the south and the fort's hospital to the west. On the north side are the granaries, the floors of which were raised on stone pillars to keep the stored grain cool and dry. The fort was built for an infantry unit of 1,000 men. Their barracks, workshops and storehouses were ranged in parallel lines on the east and west sides of the fort and in the south-east corner, against the fort wall, is the communal latrine, equipped with drains, water-channels for washing sponges, and a hand-basin. The bathhouse was on the

High Street. TONY STONE WORLDWIDE/ROB TALBOT

Housesteads fort, north granary. EH

far side of the Knag Burn, but this has yet to be excavated.

Outside the walls of the fort was an extensive civil settlement or *vicus*. The remains are barely discernible on the ground, but on an aerial photograph stand out clearly. Some of its buildings have been excavated and left exposed near the south gate, including the so-called 'Murder House' where the remains of a man and woman were found under a clay floor, the man having the point of a sword embedded in his ribs. Attached to the south gate is a small bastle house of 16th or 17th-century date which has utilised one of the guard rooms to accommodate a corn-drying kiln.

From the north-east corner of the fort the Roman wall follows the steep slope down to the Knag Burn. Near the stream is one of the few gateways through the wall independent of forts or milecastles. It has guardrooms on either side for those controlling the passage of people and goods at this border crossing.

West of the fort, within easy walking distance, is one of the miniature forts or milecastles, spaced regularly one Roman mile apart and for those wishing to explore further it is possible to continue westwards for a distance of about 3 miles (4.8km) to the next car-park at Steel Rigg (NY 751678). The walk is strenuous but exhilarating, embracing some of the best views of the Wall and its rugged surroundings.

The site museum near the fort has finds from excavations and models of the fort and other buildings. There is also an information centre at the car-park by the road.

Vindolanda fort and *vicus*. EH

Whitley Castle, CUCAP

22

Whitley Castle, Northumberland
Roman

OS 86 NY 695487. 2 miles (3.2km) N of Alston on A689. A track leads to the site on W side of road through Whitlow Farm (private property). Permission must be obtained (at the farm) before visiting the site

[B]

The fort is on the Roman road, known as Maiden Way, from Kirkby Thore (Bravoniacum) to Carvoran (Magna) just south of Hadrian's Wall. No stonework is visible but its defences are impressive and well preserved. On its west side where the ground rises steeply there are seven ramparts and ditches, and five on the north and south sides. Only Ardoch fort in Perthshire has a comparable defensive system. The fort covers an area of 3 acres (1.2ha) and, using the ground to the best advantage, is rhomboidal in shape rather than rectangular. The site of the headquarters building can be traced in uneven ground in the centre of the fort, near a field wall, and air photography has detected other buildings, including a barrack. The bath-house was outside the fort near its north-east corner.

Evidence from limited excavations and from inscriptions suggest that the fort was established in the middle of the 2nd century and continued in use until the mid-4th, with perhaps a period of rebuilding in the 3rd century. One of the inscriptions records that the garrison at one time was the Second Cohort of the Nervii, from the Lower Rhine. It has been suggested that one of the purposes of the fort was to control the lead-mining in the area and to ensure safe transit of the metal through the surrounding hills. The Roman road is on the east side of the fort. At 1,050ft (320 m) it is one of the highest Roman forts in Britain. Its Roman name is not known.

21

Vindolanda, Northumberland
Roman

OS 87 NY 770664. Bardon Mill. 2 miles (3km) SW of Housesteads Fort. Take minor road for Chesterholm off B6318, or minor road from Bardon Mill

[A] EH, Vindolanda Trust

The fort of Vindolanda lies south of the Wall on Stanegate, the road made by Agricola to link Corbridge with Carlisle. A Roman milestone stands by the roadside near the entrance to the fort and part of a second is to be found slightly more than one Roman mile to the west. Excavations have revealed a series of forts on the site, the earliest having timber defences. The first stone fort and its associated *vicus* date from the early 2nd century when the Wall defences were designed with forts behind the stone wall rather than on its line. The fort may have been modified shortly afterwards and in the early 3rd century both fort and *vicus* were extensively rebuilt. The present fort walls and gates and headquarters building were the result of this rebuilding, and west of the fort are the buildings of the reconstructed *vicus*. They include a bath-house, a *mansio*, or rest house for travellers, and buildings subdivided into rooms which have been interpreted as married quarters for troops and their families.

Many important finds have been recovered during excavations, including items of leather and wood, which usually disintegrate when buried but here were preserved by the water-logged soil. Some are on display in the site museum. Also on the site are modern full-scale reconstructions of lengths of turf and stone walls, a turret, and a milecastle gateway.

3

Early Christian Sites

Christianity was well established in Roman Britain by the end of the 4th century AD and appears to have grown in strength in the later years of Roman rule as the threat of violence and invasion became more menacing. It survived in an organised form for part of the 5th century, but as the towns declined so episcopal authority diminished, and as the heathen kingdoms of the English became more securely established in eastern and southern Britain, so Christianity was kept alive only in the north and west.

The story of the conversion of the English, beginning with the mission of Augustine to Kent in 597, is one of the most remarkable in our history. In the northern kingdom of Northumbria the first Christian mission was that of Bishop Paulinus (see 31,N) between 625 and 632. It ended with the death of King Edwin in battle, the flight of Paulinus, and a temporary return to paganism. Three years later, in 635, Aidan was summoned from the Celtic monastery of Iona by King Oswald and, establishing a monastery at Lindisfarne (38,N), completed the conversion of Northumbria which at the height of its power stretched from the Humber to the Forth and across the Pennines to the Irish Sea.

The church at Lindisfarne was built of timber, and so too was the church at the royal palace of Adgefrin at **Yeavering** (31,N). Nothing survives above ground of Aidan's monastery nor of any of the churches established during the first half of the 7th century. However, from the later years of the century there are several remarkable survivals. Parts of the monastic churches of **Monkwearmouth** (29,T) and **Jarrow** (28,T), built in stone by masons brought from the continent because native craftsmen no longer had the necessary skills, still stand, incorporated in later buildings, and at **Hexham** (27,N), Wilfrid's crypt, built about 675–80, is still intact, under the later church. These are tantalising remnants of some

of our earliest churches. At **Escomb** (25,D), however, the whole church survives. It is small and devoid of ornament, and has had minor alterations, but no building expresses more vividly the time of Bede and the character of its architecture.

At Monkwearmouth, Jarrow, and Hexham the churches were embellished with carvings and sculpture. The faint remains of a carved figure can be seen on the west front of Monkwearmouth church, and pieces of carved stonework, now detached but once part of the fabric and some bearing traces of painted decoration, have been found and preserved at all three sites. Carving of great skill and virtuosity is also to be found on the stone crosses and grave markers still surviving in considerable numbers throughout the northern counties. Pre-eminent is the high cross at **Bewcastle** (23,C), closely associated in date and style with the cross at Ruthwell across the border in south-west Scotland but once part of Northumbria. Other crosses of Anglian date are those at Hexham and **St Andrew Auckland** (30,D), at Irton (C) and Beckermet (C) and at Rothbury (N), where part of the shaft of the cross has been used to form a baptismal font. For better preservation some have been moved from churchyard to church, and others to museums. Many, however, are still in the open, eloquent witnesses of the spread of Christianity throughout the North in the 7th and 8th centuries.

In 793 Lindisfarne was sacked by Viking raiders. It was the prelude to persistent attacks on the east coast of Northumbria, as well as on the coasts further south and, later, of raids inland. In the 9th century piracy and plunder changed to permanent settlement and to the establishment about 876 of a Danish kingdom in the southern part of Northumbria with its capital in York. In the early years of the 10th century other Scandinavian settlers of Norwegian origin attacked from the west, taking control of parts of present-day Cumbria

Bewcastle cross, south and east faces. EH

and linking their territory with the Danish kingdom on the east.

In the initial attacks on Northumbria, churches and monasteries were looted and many, including those at Monkwearmouth, Jarrow and Lindisfarne, were abandoned. By the 10th century monastic life in the North had been obliterated. The Church, however, survived. The pagan newcomers were converted and assimilated, and their pagan myths absorbed into a predominantly Christian culture. The story can be traced on the later stone crosses whose carvings combine Anglian and Viking ornament and include scenes from pagan mythology, but which firmly and unmistakably are Christian monuments. They are to be found on both sides of the Pennines, but the best examples are those on the west at Penrith (C), Dearham (C), Kirkby Stephen (C) and, above all, at **Gosforth** (26,C).

23

Bewcastle, Cumbria
Late 7th century–early 8th century

OS 86 NY 566747. Bewcastle. 8 miles (12.8km) NW of Gilsland on B6318 and minor road

[A] EH (cross)

Bewcastle is more a community of scattered farms than a village, set in the bleak and windswept moorland of northern Cumbria. Historically it is one of the most interesting sites in the North. Its greatest treasure is the Bewcastle cross, but earlier than this is the Roman fort, one of the military outposts north of Hadrian's Wall and linked to the Wall by a road to Birdoswald (11,C). Its plan is an irregular hexagon within which stands the church and churchyard, the rectory, a medieval castle, and, on the northern side, a farm.

The high cross is next to the church of St Cuthbert, near its south porch. Its shaft is 14ft 6in (4.4 m) high, tapering towards the top and standing in a stone base. The original cross-head is missing.

Bewcastle cross, west face. EH

The four faces of the shaft are elaborately carved, the west face having figures of St John the Evangelist (bottom panel), Christ (middle panel), and St John the Baptist (top panel). On the east face is a vine scroll with birds and beasts. On the two narrow sides, north and south, are panels with vine scrolls, interlacing patterns, chequerwork, and on the south side, a sundial. Below the figure of Christ on the west face are eight lines of runes, the geometric alphabet of the time. Translated they are thought to commemorate Alcfrith, son of King Oswiu who ruled between 641 and 670, and on this evidence together with its stylistic treatment, the cross has been dated, not without controversy, to the late 7th century. Others consider a mid-8th-century date to be more appropriate.

Only the Ruthwell cross, across the Scottish border, is comparable in quality and completeness to this superb Christian monument. At Ruthwell the cross has been moved into the church for safe keeping; at Bewcastle it stands in the open and is in the care of English Heritage.

Bew Castle, north of the church is square in plan with high curtain walls, that on the south reaching 30ft (9.1 m) in height. There are no towers, except on the west where the entrance is within

a single tower. The living quarters were built against the curtain walls enclosing a central courtyard, but all that survives are piles of rubble. Much would be revealed by excavation. It is probably 14th-century in date.

24

Durham Cathedral, Relics of St Cuthbert, County Durham
7th century and later

OS 88 NZ 274422. Durham
[A]

St Cuthbert was one of the most venerated figures of the early church of Northumbria. He became a monk in a monastery at Melrose, moved to Lindisfarne as prior and in 685 was made bishop. He died in 687 in a hermit's cell on Farne Island and was buried in a stone sarcophagus on the right-hand side of the altar in the monastic church at Lindisfarne (38,N). Eleven years later his coffin was opened and his body found to be, in Bede's description, 'whole and uncorrupt as though still living.' It was then wrapped in a new cloak, leaving the original clothes undisturbed, and placed in a new wooden coffin which was kept

St Cuthbert's cross. DEAN AND CHAPTER OF DURHAM CATHEDRAL

on the floor of the church.

When the community was forced to leave Lindisfarne they carried Cuthbert's relics with them and eventually, in 995, settled at Durham. Here the relics have remained except for one temporary removal in 1069 when the monks feared for their lives. The coffin was re-opened in 1104, the body re-wrapped and the wooden coffin covered in a waxed cloth. It was then transferred to a shrine behind the high altar of the new cathedral where it remained, an object of wonder and pilgrimage, until the 16th century. During the Reformation the shrine was destroyed but the coffin was buried under a paving slab on the same site. In 1827 the remains were exhumed, the pieces of coffin and other relics

removed and the bones replaced in the grave.

On display in the Cathedral Treasury are the pieces of the wooden coffin in which Cuthbert was placed in 698, fragments of the burial vestments, and a small gold cross set with garnets which may have been owned and worn by Cuthbert. Also found in the coffin were an ivory comb, a small portable altar covered in silver, a 10th-century maniple and stole, and a copy of St John's Gospel, now in the library of Stonyhurst College, Lancashire. The other great manuscript associated with Lindisfarne, the Lindisfarne Gospels, written and illuminated in the monastery there, is described in the entry on Holy Island (38,N).

25

Escomb, County Durham
8th century

OS 92 NZ 189302. Escomb.
Off B6282 1½ miles (2.4km)
W of Bishop Auckland
[C]

St John's, Escomb is one of the most complete Anglo-Saxon churches in England. It is small and simple with a tall, very narrow nave and even narrower chancel, and it is astonishingly intact. No other northern building expresses more vividly the architecture and piety of the age of Bede.

Escomb church. AFK

Many of the stones probably came from the neighbouring Roman fort of Vinovia (Binchester). An inscription of the 6th Legion is built into the north wall and the chancel arch is made from re-used Roman masonry. There are original windows in the nave. The two on the south side and the one in the west gable have round heads; those on the south side are straight-headed. The north door of the nave is original though now blocked, and one jamb of the south door is also original. Saxon, too, is the north door of the chancel although it appears to be a later insertion. The lancet window is 13th-century; the larger windows date from the 19th century.

The interior has whitewashed walls and an open timber roof. After neglect and replacement by a new church in Victorian times the old church was brought back into use in 1965, its restoration and furnishing being the work of the architect, Sir Albert Edward Richardson. The font is the base of a Roman pillar. An item of great rarity is the sundial on the south wall of the nave. Visitors to Bewcastle (23,C) will see another on the south face of the high cross near the church. Other churches of the same period as Escomb are those at Monkwearmouth (29,T) and Jarrow (28,T), but they are not as complete.

26

Gosforth, Cumbria
10th century

OS 89 NY 072035. Gosforth. On A595 between Egremont and Ravenglass, on E side of village
[A]

St Mary's, Gosforth has several pieces of important pre-Conquest sculpture. Pre-eminent is the high cross in the churchyard south of the church. It stands in a stepped stone base, which is probably original, measures 14ft (4.3 m) in height, and is very slender. The shaft which is made of red sandstone is rounded in its lower part, then it becomes square. At its head is a cross within a circle. The sculptures are a

mixture of Norse mythology and Christian symbolism, as is to be expected in an area strongly influenced by Scandinavian settlement. On the east face is the Crucifixion and, above, plaited decoration linked with animals. On the west face is the pagan god Loki being cast into a pit. The north and south faces have more plaiting and animals and, on the north, another horseman. The accepted date for the cross is the first half of the 10th century.

The church is Norman in origin but was extensively rebuilt in 1896–9. At the

end of the north aisle are other sculptured stones. These include two 'hog-back' tombstones, one known as the 'Warrior's Tomb', having on one side a procession of armed men; the other, known as the 'Saint's Tomb', has carvings of crucifixions on its two ends. Their curved 'roofs' and boat-shaped sides are typical of this type of monument, found in the areas of Scandinavian settlement in the north of England, and with the greatest concentration in Cumbria and the northern parts of Yorkshire. Another

Gosforth cross. T MIDDLEMASS/BRITISH ACADEMY

carved stone in the church depicts a boat with fishermen, and was possibly part of a wall panel or frieze.

Other crosses and sculptured stones in the area are at Irton and Beckermet, both near Gosforth; at Cross Canonby, near Maryport; and at Aspatria, between Maryport and Wigton.

27

Hexham Abbey, Wilfrid's Crypt, Northumberland
7th century

OS 87 NY 935642. Hexham. Off A69 between Newcastle and Carlisle
[C]

The first church at Hexham was built by Wilfrid, abbot of Ripon and, from 669, bishop of all Northumbria, on land given by Queen Aethelthryth between 671 and 673. According to Wilfrid's biographer it was the most splendid church north of the Alps, great in size and richly decorated. The only substantial part still remaining is its crypt. Hexham was sacked by the Danes in 876, and in 1113 an Augustine priory was founded on the same site.

Entrance to the crypt is down a modern flight of steps in the nave of the priory church. At the bottom is a small vestibule and directly in front is the relic chamber, tunnel-vaulted and still with some of its original plaster on the walls. There are passages on either side of the chamber, each, originally, with its own staircase. The north staircase and passage, which leads to the vestibule, is thought to have been for worshippers, while the south passage, which has a door into the relic chamber, probably was for priests. Many of the stones are Roman and have carved inscriptions. One of them, at the end of the north passage, is a re-used Roman altar.

Below the choir of the church the foundations of an early apse have been found, and at floor level, above the apse, is a remarkable 7th-century stone chair, possibly once the seat of the bishop. Within the church are several pieces of Anglo-Saxon sculpture including, in the south transept, an 8th-century cross,

Hexham Abbey crypt. RCHME

thought to commemorate Acca, bishop of Hexham, who died in 740. In the south transept is a Roman tombstone dedicated to a cavalry officer, Flavinus, and in the passage outside the south doorway are two Roman altars.

A crypt closely comparable to the one at Hexham is to be found at Ripon in North Yorkshire, under the nave of Ripon Minster. Like the Hexham crypt it is the only surviving part of a monastic church built by Wilfrid in the 7th century.

28

Jarrow Monastery, Tyne and Wear
7th century and later

OS 88 NZ 339652. Jarrow. On S bank of River Tyne, on minor road N of A185
[C] EH (ruins)

Jarrow monastery is the sister house of the monastery at Wearmouth (Monkwearmouth, 29,T). It was founded by Benedict Biscop, abbot of Wearmouth, on land given in 681–2 by the same donor, King Ecgfrith of Northumbria. When established they were thought of as two parts of the same

monastery. The first monks at Jarrow came from Wearmouth with their prior, Ceolfrid, and by 685 their church, dedicated to St Paul, was ready for use. The dedication stone over the chancel arch in the present church reads:

DEDICATIO BASILICAE
SCI PAULI VIIII KL MAI
ANNO XV ECFRIDI REG
CEOLFRIDI ABB EIUSDEM Q
Q ECCLES DO AUCTORE
CONDITORES ANNO IIII

(The dedication of the basilica of St Paul on the 9th day before the kalends of May [i.e. 23 April] in the 15th year of King Ecgfrith and in the 4th year of Abbot Ceolfrid founder by the guidance of God of the same church.)

Originally the monastery had two churches positioned end-to-end but with a space dividing the two. Only one of these survives, the east church, and this is now the chancel of the present building. It is tall and narrow, like the churches at Escomb (25,D) and Monkwearmouth, and much of its original walling survives, made of carefully laid, squared stones. There are three original windows in the south wall, two of them filled with stone panels pierced with small circular openings filled with glass, and a blocked original doorway in the north wall. The larger windows are later in date.

The west church was larger and more elaborate. It had a nave and chancel, a two-storey west porch, and *porticus* or side-chapels north and south of the nave. This church, almost certainly the one dedicated to St Paul, and the first on the site, was demolished in 1782 and eventually replaced by the present nave and aisle built in 1866 to the designs of Sir George Gilbert Scott. The domestic buildings of the monastery were to the south of the two churches and are marked out on the ground. Excavation has discovered two stone buildings parallel with the churches, one possibly a refectory and the other a hall with a small, two-room lodging at one end, but their remains are below present ground level.

Like Wearmouth, Jarrow was abandoned in the 9th century and not

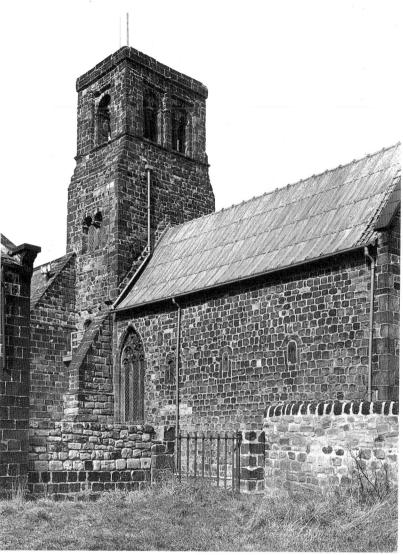

St Paul's church, Jarrow. RCHME

History of the English Church and People. He died here in May 735 and was buried in the church, but between 1020 and 1041 his bones were removed and placed in the tomb of St Cuthbert at Durham (24,D).

In Jarrow Hall, 300 yards (273 m) north of the church, the Bede Monastery Museum has exhibitions about the monastery, and objects found during excavations are on display.

29

Monkwearmouth Monastery, Tyne and Wear
7th century and later

OS 88 NZ 402578. Sunderland. On N bank of River Wear on A1018. From the bridge follow road signs and giratory road system
[C]

The monastery at Wearmouth, now Monkwearmouth, was founded by Benedict Biscop, a Northumbrian nobleman who travelled abroad, became a monk at the island monastery of Lérins off the coast of France, and returned to England in 669 to become abbot of the monastery of St Peter and St Paul at Canterbury. About 673 Benedict visited the court of King Ecgfrith of Northumbria and was given land by the king to establish a new monastic community on the north bank of the River Wear, near a small harbour. Building began in 674 and, because the required skills were not available in Britain, masons were brought from France to build a church of stone, and glaziers imported to provide glass for the windows. The church was completed in 675 and dedicated to St Peter.

All that survives of the monastery is the west wall and the west porch of this church. Judging from these remains, and piecing together the evidence from excavations, the church was tall and narrow like Escomb (25,D) and had at its east end a chancel or, possibly, a chapel dedicated to St Mary. There is evidence of a *porticus* or side-chapel on the north side of the nave, and perhaps a corresponding one on the south side. At

refounded until after the Norman Conquest. With the return of monastic life the churches were restored, and probably at this time the tower linking the two churches was built, although some believe that the base of the tower is older. New living quarters were built on the site of the old but at a higher level, the area south of the church being raised and terraced to provide space for a more regular claustral arrangement. However, although a full complement of monastic buildings may have been intended, only east and south ranges

were built and for much of its history Jarrow remained a small Benedictine community dependent on Durham and with a limited number of monks in residence. Again there is a close parallel with Wearmouth monastery. After closure in the 16th century the domestic parts of the monastery were used as a house, and a cottage built against the west wall was in occupation into the 20th century.

Jarrow was the home of the scholar and historian, Bede. It was here that he wrote one of his greatest works, the

the west end, attached to the west wall, was a two-storeyed porch which now forms the lower part of the tower and whose gable can be seen in changes in the masonry. At ground floor level the porch is tunnel-vaulted and has a round-headed doorway with pairs of balusters standing on plinths carved with thin intertwined beasts, badly eroded but still just discernible. Originally the porch had small single-storey chambers on either side but these have not survived.

The domestic quarters of the monastery lay to the south of the church and traces have been found by excavation. Nothing remains above ground. The monastery was attacked by Vikings in 793 and abandoned in the 9th century. It was refounded shortly after the Norman Conquest but by this time the church was roofless and in ruins, and the other buildings uninhabitable. The monastery was rebuilt and a small Benedictine community established here as a dependency of Durham. It was closed in 1536 and the domestic parts made into a house. This burned down in the 18th century and subsequently the

site was cleared. In the 19th century the area became part of a suburb of Sunderland.

The present church has a 14th-century chancel and a 19th-century north aisle and chapel. The upper part of the west tower is 11th-century. Fragments of carvings and other architectural details recovered by excavation are on display in the parish hall at the east end of the church. Others are in Sunderland Museum and in the Monks' Dormitory at Durham. The history of Wearmouth monastery is closely linked with that of Jarrow (28,T) which was founded about eight years later by the same Benedict Biscop.

30
St Andrew Auckland, County Durham
Late 8th–Early 9th century

OS 93 NZ 217284. St Andrew Auckland. 1 mile (1.6km) SE of Bishop Auckland on A6072 and B6282

[C]

St Andrew's church is a 13th-century collegiate church with some of its collegiate buildings still surviving although converted to other uses (East Deanery, now a farm). Notable features of the church are the two-storeyed south porch and the 15th-century chancel stalls. Within the church is a cross shaft and base, later than those at Bewcastle (23,C) and Ruthwell (in Dumfries and Galloway in Scotland) and less well preserved but still impressive. The surviving pieces were found during an 1881 restoration of the church, and the cross was reconstructed in 1938 replacing missing parts with stone and concrete. On the front in the central panel is a crucifixion, thought to be of St Andrew, with two figures with halos in the panel on the base. The sides have birds and animals entangled in leafy scrolls, and an archer shooting at the birds. The carving is bold and vigorous and the cross is thought to date from about 800. (Illustrated page 34.)

St Peter's church, Monkwearmouth. J ALLAN CASH

Cross in St Andrew's church, St Andrew
Auckland. RCHME

Artist's impression of Yeavering. EH

31

Yeavering, Northumberland
6th and 7th centuries

OS 75 NT 925306. Wooler. B6351
from Wooler to Old Yeavering. Site
notice at roadside

[D]

In his *History of the English Church
and People*, completed in 731, Bede tells
the story of the conversion of King
Edwin of Northumbria, and many of his

people, by Bishop Paulinus, who was
sent from Canterbury in 625 to bring
Christianity to the North. Edwin was
baptised in York on the eve of Easter Day
627, in a wooden church built for the
occasion, and afterwards Paulinus
'preached the word throughout the
country.' At some time after 627
Paulinus is said to have accompanied the
king and queen to the royal palace of
Adgefrin and to have stayed there for
thirty-six days, 'constantly occupied in
instructing and baptizing.' During this
period, according to Bede, 'he did

nothing from dawn to dusk but proclaim
Christ's saving message to the people,
who gathered from all the surrounding
villages and countryside; and when he
had instructed them he washed them in
the cleansing waters of Baptism in the
near-by River Glen.'

Adgefrin had long been identified
with Yeavering, at the foot of Yeavering
Bell and close to the River Glen, but its
exact position was not known. In 1949 a
potential site was located by aerial
photography, and from 1953 to 1962 the
site was excavated. The investigations

revealed a series of great halls built of timber, also an open-air meeting place with tiered seating in front of a platform or throne, and a great palisaded enclosure, not around the buildings but to one side. One of the smaller buildings was identified as a church, which appears to have replaced a pagan temple and to have become the focus of a Christian cemetery.

None of these remains can be seen on the ground. Evidence of the buildings was provided by post-holes and slots in the soil under the surface, which had to be re-buried on completion of the work. Nevertheless, the story they revealed makes the site one of great historical importance. It appears to have been in use before the coming of the English and to have been taken over and developed by the English kings as a royal palace where councils and assemblies were held, and where the king and his court stayed during royal progresses. It has been suggested that the pagan temple was cleansed by Paulinus and used by him during his stay, and that the church was built during the reign of

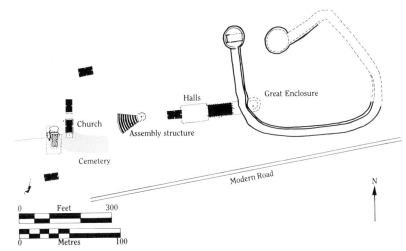

Yeavering (after B Hope-Taylor). EH

Edwin's successor, King Oswald.

Edwin was slain in 632 and on his death Paulinus returned to Canterbury, although one of his companions, James the Deacon, stayed in the area. For a time paganism triumphed, but in 635 King Oswald invited Aidan to Lindisfarne and the Christian message was spread again through the North, although initially by Celtic missionaries from Lindisfarne (38,N) rather than from Canterbury. Adgefrin was rebuilt and continued in use until the late-7th century but then was abandoned in favour of 'Maelmin', which is Milfield, 2 miles (3.2km) to the north.

4

Places of Worship

The greatest churches of the northern counties are those of the former monasteries. Pre-eminent is Durham (24 and 66,D), church of a Benedictine priory until the Dissolution, as well as cathedral of the diocese. Carlisle (65,C), too, was both a priory church and cathedral, and throughout the area are many other monastic churches, some continuing in use as parish churches, others wantonly destroyed on the order of Henry VIII in the 16th century, and remaining only as ruins.

One of the most complete, after Durham, is the church of **Cartmel Priory** (35,C), partially unroofed in the 16th century but later restored in its entirety to serve as the parish church of its community. Complete, too, are the churches of **Brinkburn Priory** (33,N), restored from ruin in the 19th century, and that of Hexham Abbey (27,N), which has its medieval eastern parts still surviving, but a nave of 1907–9, replacing one destroyed by the Scots in 1296.

Other monastic churches less complete but still in use are those at **Lanercost** (39,C) and Holme Cultram (C), while entirely ruinous are the great churches of the former monasteries at **Furness** (36,C), **Shap** (41,C), Egglestone (D), Finchale (D), Tynemouth (59,T), and Lindisfarne (38,N), all testifying to the intense and widespread religious life of the early Middle Ages which saw old sites such as Jarrow (28,T) and Monkwearmouth (29,T) revived, and many new monasteries founded in the remote valleys of the North.

Later, and mainly in the towns, came the friars. Among their several, but seldom surviving, foundations are the Dominican friary in Newcastle (71,T) and the Carmelite friary at Hulne (N), one now partially restored and the other an eloquent ruin.

The only complete pre-Conquest church is Escomb (25,D), a precious survival, but other churches with some pre-Conquest work are those at **Bywell** (34,N), Corbridge (77,N), Ovingham (N), Whittingham (N) and Morland (C). Few churches were built in the early years of Norman rule but 12th-century work is to be found at Norham (57,N) and Warkworth (60,N), both new boroughs founded in the 12th century, and also at Seaton Delaval (94,N), Edlingham (N), Heddon-on-the-Wall (N) and Chollerton (N), where the south arcade has re-used Roman columns, probably taken from the fort at Chesters, a few miles to the south. Heighington (D) is largely 12th-century and, in Cumbria, where examples are scarce, the parish church of Kirkby Lonsdale has bold and powerful arcades, inspired probably by Durham Cathedral.

Outstanding churches of the later 12th and 13th centuries are St Cuthbert's, Darlington (D), begun about 1190 and virtually complete by 1250, St Andrew's church at St Andrew Auckland (30,D), All Saints, Lanchester (D), the church of Holy Cross, Haltwhistle (N) and St Aidan's church at Bamburgh (48,N).

After 1300 the Border suffered 300 years of turmoil and warfare, and few churches were built. Some strong towers, whose main role was to provide a refuge, were added to existing buildings for example at Newton Arlosh (80,C), Burgh by Sands (C), Great Salkeld (C) and Ancroft (N), while a few late-medieval churches were built in the more prosperous towns. St Nicholas's church, Newcastle, made cathedral of the diocese in 1882, is one of the largest of these; others are at Kendal (68,C), Appleby (61,C) and Alnwick (47,N).

There is virtually nothing from the Tudor period and little from the 17th century. Holy Trinity, Berwick (49,N), built between 1650 and 1652 is a notable exception and, slightly later, the redoubtable Lady Anne Clifford rebuilt St Ninian's church at Brougham (50,C) in 1660, and St Wilfrid's chapel in the same parish. St Ninian's has furnishings of Lady Anne's time but St Wilfrid's was re-equipped in the 19th century with woodwork from several European

Durham cathedral from the south-west. AFK

Door knocker, Durham cathedral. AFK

countries and of various dates. The chancel of St Lawrence's church, Appleby is also Lady Anne's work. A precious survival in this church is an organ case, acquired from Carlisle cathedral in 1684 and thought to contain 16th-century work.

Other woodwork of exceptional interest is that inspired by Bishop Cosin, bishop of Durham from 1662 to 1672. Earlier he was vicar of Brancepeth (D) and here, as well as in several other churches, he introduced pews, pulpits, screens, and choir stalls, made by local craftsmen and carved in an exuberant mixture of styles, part gothic and part classical. St Edmund's, Sedgefield (D) has Cosin woodwork, as has the chapel at the bishop's palace, **Bishop Auckland** (32,D), where Cosin is buried. In Durham Cathedral are choir stalls, screens, and a stupendous font cover 40ft (12.2 m) tall and 9ft (2.7 m) wide at the base, given by him.

In the 18th century church building revived and several towns have good churches of the period with original interiors. Among the best are those at Sunderland (St John's, built in 1719 and enlarged in 1745), Penrith (St Andrew's, 1720–2), Whitehaven (St James's, 1752–3, 106,C), Newcastle (St Ann's, 1768 and All Saints, 1786–96), and Carlisle (St Cuthbert's, 1778). Also 18th-century in date are a number of Lakeland churches, generally modest in size and appearance, such as those at Mungrisdale (C) and Threlkeld (C), built when large

parishes were divided into smaller, more manageable units.

19th-century churches are plentiful both in the towns, which needed new churches to meet their ever increasing populations, and in the country, where often little had been built since the early-Middle Ages. Gothic was the preferred style but there are exceptions, such as St Mary's, Wreay (C), 5 miles (8km) south of Carlisle, designed in an Italian Romanesque style by Miss Sara Losh in memory of her sister, and consecrated in 1842. Firmly gothic is St Mary's, Dalton-in-Furness (C), a handsome late-Victorian building by Paley and Austin (1882–5), and still gothic, although more individual in style is St Andrew's, **Roker** (40,T) designed by E S Prior and built in 1906–7.

Non-conformist chapels and meeting houses are many and widespread. Among the earliest is the Quaker meeting house at **Swarthmoor** near Ulverston (42,C), built in 1688 on land given by George Fox, founder of the movement; others are to be found in the same locality where Quakerism took root and spread with vigour, defying early persecution. Examples of 18th-century chapels, Congregational (46,C),

Baptist (43,D), Presbyterian (45,C), and Methodist (44,D), are gathered at the end of this chapter, selected mainly because of their early foundation. They represent the very large number still existing throughout the area, often small and simple when in remote parts, larger and more ostentatious in their urban form.

32

Bishop Auckland, Chapel of the Bishop's Palace, County Durham
Middle Ages and 17th century

OS 93 NZ 215301. Bishop Auckland. On N side of town on A689

[C]

The chapel was formerly the great hall of the palace. It was begun about 1190 in the time of Bishop Pudsey and consists of a long rectangular hall divided into nave and aisles. The arches of the arcades and half the shafts of the quatrefoil piers are of Frosterley marble from Weardale. The aisle windows date from the early 14th century, put in during alterations

Chapel of the Bishop's Palace, Bishop Auckland. RCHME

by Bishop Bek, but the tracery was restored in the 19th century.

Conversion from hall to chapel was the work of Bishop Cosin. Cosin began his career as chaplain to the bishop in 1619, became a prebendary of the cathedral in 1624, and vicar of Brancepath from 1626 to 1635. During and after the Civil War he spent thirteen years abroad, returning to England at the Restoration to become bishop of Durham from 1662 to 1672. Architecturally he is remembered in particular for some remarkable church woodwork, which in the earlier pieces combines traditional gothic style with 17th-century motifs and ornament, and later becomes more baroque. It is to be seen in many of the buildings with which he was associated.

At Bishop Auckland he added the clerestory, refaced the south front, and furnished the interior. The panelled ceiling is his, as are the screen, the chancel stalls, and the pulpit and reading desk. The Father Smith organ dates from 1688. Bishop Cosin is buried here and is commemorated by a plain black marble slab in the middle of the floor. The monument by Nollekens is for Bishop Trevor who died in 1771. In the park is an unusually elaborate deer shelter built by Bishop Trevor in 1760. Its architectural elaboration will make a visit worthwhile.

33

Brinkburn Priory, Northumberland
12th–13th centuries and later

OS 81 NZ 116984. Rothbury. 25 miles (40km) NW of Newcastle on A1, A697 and B6344, 4½ miles (7km) SE of Rothbury

[A] EH

Brinkburn priory was founded about 1135 by William Bertram, lord of Mitford. He established a community of Augustinian canons in a secluded part of the Coquet valley, by the side of the river and at the foot of steep slopes. It still has an air of remoteness, and the surroundings are remarkably beautiful.

Brinkburn Priory. EH

Throughout its history the priory was only modestly endowed and its property was further reduced by Scottish raids in the 14th century and by robbery. It was closed in 1536 but the church was kept in repair until well into the 17th century and used for services. Thereafter it fell into ruin and remained so for nearly 200 years. In the early part of the 19th century a house was built on the site of the south range of the priory by Richard Hodgson and in the middle of the century his grandson, Cadogan Hodgson

Cadogan, began to restore the church, with Thomas Austin of Newcastle as architect. Work began in 1858 and was completed in 1868. Except for the south-west corner of the nave and parts of the gables, most of the walls were standing, so much of the restoration was a matter of repair and refacing rather than providing new parts. However, the roofs are entirely new and so are some of the architectural details, such as the gable window in the south transept. Changes were also made above the north aisle of the nave and above the chancel where chambers, inserted in the 14th century, were not reinstated.

The church is cruciform in plan with a short, square eastern end, aisled transept, and a nave with an aisle on the north side only, like Lanercost (39,C). It was started towards the end of the 12th century and completed in the first part of the 13th, with the architectural detail becoming more thoroughly Early English the further west it proceeded. The most exuberant decoration is on the north doorway. The organ of 1868 was the gift of Sir William Armstrong of Cragside, and so too was the bell over the north transept.

34

Bywell, Northumberland
Anglo-Saxon, Middle Ages and later

OS 87 NZ 049615. Bywell. Off A695 12 miles (19km) W of Newcastle on A695 or A69 and minor roads

[C] (St Peter)   [A] Redundant Churches Fund (St Andrew)

Bywell has two churches but no village. In the 16th century it was a thriving

community 'inhabyted with handy craftsmen whose trade is all in yron worke', and there were twenty houses still occupied in the early 19th century. Now it is predominantly parkland belonging to Bywell Hall.

The two churches stand close together and both are Anglo-Saxon in origin. St Andrew's has a fine late-Saxon tower with large belfry openings on all four sides of its upper stage, and smaller round-headed windows below. Differences in the stonework suggest that the lower part may have been an early west porch, like that at Corbridge (77,N), rebuilt when the height was increased to make a tower. Below the belfry opening on the south side is a doorway and inside the church there is evidence of an opening into the nave at first floor level. The rest of St Andrew's is mainly 13th-century but chancel and north transept were rebuilt in the 19th century. In the chancel is part of a cross-shaft with interlace carving.

The evidence of St Peter's early date is internal. The nave walls and the western part of the chancel are Anglo-Saxon and archaeologists believe there were side-chapels or *porticus* on the north and south sides, overlapping the nave and chancel. The evidence for a northern chapel is a blocked doorway in

the north wall of the chancel and a roofing scar on the outside of the wall. The remains of a south chapel are more difficult to detect. The tower, south arcade, and eastern part of the chancel are 13th-century. The present north chapel is mid-14th-century.

At Ovingham, 2 miles (3.25km) to the east, the tower of St Mary's church has architectural detail very similar to that of St Andrew's.

35

Cartmel Priory, Cumbria
Middle Ages and later

OS 96 SD 380788. Cartmel. By minor road from Grange-over-Sands on B5277

[C] NT (priory gatehouse)

The priory was founded in 1188 by William Marshal, lord of Cartmel and later earl of Pembroke, for a community of Augustinian canons. Originally their cloister and living quarters were on the south side of the church, but in the 15th century, for reasons that are not known, they were moved to the north side. None of the domestic buildings survive except for the 14th-century priory gatehouse which stands in the square. From 1624 to 1790 it housed the town's grammar school.

As part of the foundation William Marshal stipulated that an altar should be provided within the priory church for the people of Cartmel and in 1537 this saved the church from destruction. The priory was closed, the canons dispersed, and the roofs stripped, except for the south aisle which became the parish church of Cartmel. The rest of the building was abandoned until George Preston of Holker Hall (89,C), who had acquired some of the priory's lands, paid for the re-roofing of the church and gave it the carved screen at the west end of the chancel and the wooden canopies over the choir stalls. The stalls themselves and their fine misericords are 15th-century.

The eastern parts of the church, the crossing, and the transepts date from the first period of building, between

St Peter's church, Bywell. RCHME

Cartmell Priory. AFK

1190 and 1220, but the windows are later including the splendid east window which is 15th-century and retains some of its original glass. Also 15th-century are the nave and the upper part of the tower which is placed diagonally, apparently for structural reasons. The south doorway in the nave is part of the early church and has an elaborately carved round arch.

In the south chapel is the 14th-century tomb of John, Lord Harrington and Joan his wife, which has clusters of carved figures on its base, and traces of original painting on the wooden ceiling under the canopy. Two other monuments are worth noting. The first is one with the Preston coat of arms and an inscription recording the restoration of the church by George Preston. The second is the tomb of Lord Frederick Cavendish, murdered by extremists in Phoenix Park, Dublin, in 1882. The effigy is by Thomas Woolner, one of the original members of the Pre-Raphaelite Brotherhood.

36

Furness Abbey, Cumbria
Middle Ages

OS 96 SD 218717. Barrow-in-Furness. 1½ miles (2.4km) NE of Barrow-in-Furness, on A590 and minor road

[A] EH

In 1124 Stephen, count of Boulogne and later king of England, founded an abbey at Tulketh near Preston in Lancashire. It was affiliated to the Order of Savigny, a newly established order of monks which started in Normandy. Three years later Stephen moved the brethren to Furness, and in 1147, with an amalgamation of two orders, Furness became a Cistercian monastery. It was given a generous

endowment and over the years its properties and wealth increased to the point that at the time of its closure in 1537 it was the second richest Cistercian monastery in England, exceeded only by Fountains Abbey in North Yorkshire.

The site museum stands on the edge of the outer court and close to it are the remains of the abbey's outer gatehouse, by the roadside. So, walking towards the abbey, one passes through the outer court which once contained barns, storehouses, stables and workshops, as well as guest-houses whose remains are on the left. In front is the abbey church, parts of which stand almost to full height. The eastern arm was rebuilt and enlarged in the 15th century but the crossing and lower parts of the transepts date from the 12th century. On the south wall of the presbytery is a fine sedilia and piscina. At the west end of the nave is the bell tower, built about 1500, partly within the church because useable space was limited.

The domestic buildings around the cloister include a very long east range with the monks' dormitory occupying the upper floor, and, at ground level, the chapter house which retained its vaulting until as late as the 18th century. The refectory was on the south side of the cloister, at first parallel with the church but later at right angles and rebuilt on a much larger scale. On the west side of the cloister were the quarters of the lay brethren who undertook most of the manual work needed by the community. Their refectory and kitchen were at ground level and their dormitory on the floor above. Further to the south was the infirmary which had its own chapel and kitchen, and across the stream to the east are the remains of the abbot's house, which was made from an earlier infirmary. The careful planning of water supplies and drainage channels is a feature of monastic planning, and it is especially evident at Furness. Another necessary adjunct was a precinct wall to give privacy and some protection. On most sites it has been robbed for use in other buildings, but Furness still has considerable lengths surviving, especially on the eastern slopes of the valley.

After closure and the removal of the most valuable items by royal officials the abbey passed into private hands. In the 17th century a house was built by Sir Thomas Preston on the site now occupied by the museum and car park, and rebuilt in the 19th century as a hotel for the railway. Part still remains, presently used as a restaurant.

The abbey developed a harbour on Walney Island to promote its trade in wool and iron, and built a castle at Piel (C) for its protection. At Dalton (C) 2 miles (3.25km) north of the abbey is a 14th-century tower which was used by the abbey as an administrative centre and court house.

37

Gibside Chapel, Tyne and Wear
18th century and later

OS 88 NZ 172583. Burnopfield.
6 miles (9.6km) SW of Gateshead on B6314 between Rowlands Gill and Burnopfield

[A] NT

The chapel is part of the Gibside estate many of whose buildings, including the house, are ruinous. It was designed by James Paine, begun in 1760, and

intended as the mausoleum of the Bowes family, owners of the property. It is in the form of a Greek cross, namely with each arm of equal length, with a dome over the central space supported on giant Corinthian columns, and four much smaller domes over the corner spaces.

At the centre of the chapel is the communion table within a railed enclosure and to its east a splendid three-decker pulpit with a sounding board over the top tier. The side spaces have box pews and there are more pews in three of the corner areas. The fourth contains the font.

The chapel was not finished until

Furness Abbey. EH

1810, and consecrated in 1812. Much of the decorative detail is of this time. It was restored in 1965 while in the care of the National Trust.

The grounds were landscaped by 'Capability' Brown, and from the chapel a long avenue extends to a column put up by George Bowes in the 1750s. It is higher than Nelson's Column and carries a 12ft high statue (3.6 m) of British Liberty as a grandiloquent political gesture. Also in the grounds is the Banqueting House, a fanciful gothick building designed by Daniel Garrett in 1751. It was restored in 1980 by the Landmark Trust and is now a holiday cottage.

38

Holy Island, Northumberland
12th–20th centuries

OS 75 NU 126418. Berwick-upon-Tweed. 6 miles (9.6km) E of A1 across causeway at low tide. It is essential to note tide tables at ends of causeway before crossing

[A] EH, NT

Lindisfarne, later known as Holy Island, is one of the great Christian centres of England. It was the home of the first monastery in northern England, founded on the island in 635 by Aidan, a monk from Iona in the Inner Hebrides. Aidan was summoned by King Oswald of Northumbria to convert his people to Christianity and, according to the historian Bede, Aidan and his fellow priests 'proclaimed the word of God with great devotion in all the provinces under Oswald's rule . . . Churches were built in several places and people flocked gladly to hear the word of God, while the King of his bounty gave money and lands to establish monasteries.' Aidan's monastery was small and primitive. It consisted of a few huts of timber and thatch clustered round a small church and surrounded by a low bank and ditch. Its site is not known but it may have been somewhere near the present monastery, built five centuries later. In the museum are grave markers and cross shafts belonging to the early

Gibside chapel. RCHME

Lindisfarne Priory, Holy Island. EH

monastery, the earliest dating from about 700.

Among the bishops who succeeded Aidan were Cuthbert, whose tomb became an object of pilgrimage and veneration, and Eadfrith who, about

698, wrote and illuminated the Lindisfarne Gospels, one of the world's greatest treasures, now in the British Library in London. In 793 Lindisfarne was attacked by Vikings and the surviving monks left the island taking with them the body of Cuthbert. They moved first to Norham (N), then to Chester-le-Street (D), and finally to Durham (24 and 66,D) about the year 995.

The present remains on Lindisfarne are those of a Benedictine priory built in the 12th century, probably by masons from Durham. The church consists of a nave with aisles, north and south transepts with a tower over the crossing and, originally, a round-ended chancel, later extended and rebuilt with a square end. The church was vaulted throughout and the round columns of the nave have incised geometrical patterns which are very similar to those of Durham Cathedral.

The domestic buildings of the monks were on the south side of the church and follow the usual pattern of east, south and west ranges enclosing a cloister with the church on the fourth side. Of particular interest, however, is the south range where, because of declining numbers, the monks' refectory was converted in the 14th century into a large hall with rooms at one end and service quarters at the other, exactly like a secular house. Remarkable, too, is the survival of the outer court which

contains a guesthouse, stables, a vat, a well, and kiln, probably for corn drying. Notice also the battlemented walls of the outer court, the fortified tower at the end of the south range, the barbican in front of the cloister entrance, and the arrow slits in the west wall of the church, all built by the monks for their protection against Scottish raids.

The priory was closed in 1537 and during the 16th century its buildings were used as military storehouses. Gradually it fell into disrepair and between 1780 and 1820 the nave and central tower collapsed.

From the 16th century onwards the island was garrisoned and fortifications built to protect its harbour. One of these is Osborne's Fort on a promontory on the south-west side of the harbour. It dates from the 1670s and had a central tower with musket loops within an outer wall. Another, earlier fortification was on the rock to the north-east, now the site of Lindisfarne Castle. The 'castle' is the work of Edwin Lutyens who converted the 16th-century gun batteries and guardrooms into a house for Edward Hudson in 1903. It is an exciting building whether viewed from a distance with rock and castle rising out

of the sea, or explored at close quarters. The rooms are small but the ingenuity of the planning, the manipulation of space, and the quality of the fittings, make it a masterpiece of architectural design. It is now in the care of the National Trust.

North of the castle is a walled garden designed by Lutyen's colleague and adviser, Gertrude Jekyll. To the east, below the castle, is a group of lime kilns built in 1860 and in use until 1900. Lime was shipped from here to the mainland. In the village, St Mary's church, mainly of the 12th and 13th centuries, and the priory museum are both worth visiting.

39

Lanercost Priory, Cumbria
Middle Ages

OS 86 NY 556637. Brampton.
2 miles (3.2km) NE of Brampton
by minor road off A69

[A] EH

The priory of St Mary Magdalene was founded about 1166 for Augustinian canons by Robert de Vaux, lord of Gilsland. It has a beautiful setting beside the River Irthing but, close to the border, it was open to attack from the Scots and severely damaged on three occasions, in 1296, 1297 and 1346. The principal surviving part is the 13th-century nave of the abbey church. After closure of the priory in 1537 the north aisle was used as the parish church, and in 1740 the whole of the nave, which had become derelict, was restored to use. The present roof, pews and organ case were the gift of Rosalind, countess of Carlisle, in the 19th century. The eastern parts of the church also survive, but these are roofless. They contain the tombs of the Dacres and Howards, of Naworth (56,C).

The monastic quarters lay to the south of the church. Little remains of the east range, but on the south side of the cloister is the *cellarium* where the priory's stores were kept. It has a fine stone vault and now houses a collection of Roman altars and medieval carvings. Above the vault, at first floor level, was the refectory. The west range was made

Lanercost Priory. AFK

44

St Andrew's church, Roker. EDWIN SMITH

into a private house at the Dissolution by Sir Thomas Dacre of Naworth. Formerly it was the prior's lodging. At its south end is a pele tower, built to provide a measure of protection. The roofed part of the west range is used as the parish hall.

Edward I visited Lanercost three times. On the third occasion, mortally ill, he was obliged to stay for six months. On his way from Lanercost to Scotland he died at Burgh by Sands (C) on the Solway Firth. A monument stands near the site. While at Lanercost the king and some of his retinue were probably accommodated in the guest house, now the vicarage, near the west front.

Notice the lovely 13th-century statue of St Mary Magdalene high on the west front, and the remains of the priory's outer gatehouse by the roadside. Lanercost bridge, now free from road traffic, is 16th-century in date. The medieval crossing was further upstream.

40

Roker, St Andrew's Church, Tyne and Wear
Early 20th century

OS 88 NZ 404593. Sunderland. On side road off A183 1½ miles (2.4km) NE of city centre, on N side of River Wear

[C]

St Andrew's church was built in 1906–7 to the design of E S Prior. It was paid for by John Priestman, a self-made millionaire, and sited in a new suburb of Sunderland. It is cruciform in plan with a tower, not over the crossing, nor at the west end, but sitting astride the chancel. The tower is buttressed, and along the nave are other buttresses, stepped and gabled, which internally support immense arches spanning the nave and springing from almost ground level. The windows have gothic tracery, but simplified and angular.

Its fittings are by designers of the Arts and Crafts movement inspired by William Morris. The woodwork is by Ernest Gimson, stained glass by H A Payne, lettering by Eric Gill, and the tapestry used as a reredos was designed by Edward Burne-Jones and woven by Morris and Co. The painted decorations

Shap Abbey. EH

Friends meeting house, Swarthmoor. LIBRARY OF THE SOCIETY OF FRIENDS

of the chancel were designed by Prior. It is an unusual building, rooted in the gothic tradition but in both form and detail highly original. It is one of the best churches of its period.

41

Shap Abbey, Cumbria
Middle Ages

OS 90 NY 548153. Shap. 1½ miles (2.4km) W of Shap, on minor road off A6, on N side of village

[A] EH

The abbey was first established at Preston Patrick, near Kendal, by Thomas, son of Gospatric, a local landowner. Before 1201 it was moved to its present site, tucked away in the fells by the side of the River Lowther. The community belonged to the Premonstratensian Order whose rule allowed its members to work outside the abbey, for example as parish priests. They were commonly known as 'white canons' because of their dress. In the northern counties other abbeys of this order were founded at Egglestone (D), at Alnwick (47,N) and at Blanchland (63,N). Little is known about the history of the abbey. Its most famous member was Abbot Robert Redman who became bishop of St Asaph, then of Exeter, and finally of Ely. It was closed in 1540 during the Dissolution of the monasteries ordered by Henry VIII.

Most of the buildings are now only low walls. The exception is the bell tower at the west end of the church, built about 1500. The church, on the north side of the cloister, was built in the 13th century but lengthened in the 15th century at the east end, by one bay. The circles in the nave pavement mark the positions taken by the canons after the Sunday procession round the buildings. East of the cloister was the dormitory, on the upper floor above the sacristy, chapter house and warming house. In the south range was the dining hall (refectory), again on the upper floor. In the lower part of the west range the cellarer kept the abbey's stores; the floor above was probably the abbot's lodging.

Additional walls and vaults were built inside this range in the 14th century, a time of general insecurity, perhaps to strengthen it against attack.

Reredorter (latrine block) and infirmary are to the south-east, near the river. Masonry channels to flush the latrines survive in the river bed, near the bank, and there are the remains of a penstock to regulate the flow of water through the channels. Outside the infirmary is a rectangular stone-lined tank with a waste hole at the bottom. Its skilful construction suggests the work of a medieval mason, but its use is not known.

42

Swarthmoor Meeting House, Cumbria
Late 17th century

OS 96 SD 283770. Ulverston. 1 mile (1.6km) S of Ulverston on A590 and minor road

[C]

On the porch of the meeting house is a stone carved with the letters and date EX DONO G: F: 1688. It commemorates the gift by George Fox, founder of the Quaker movement, of land and money

for the building of this meeting house, one of the earliest in the country. Fox first visited the area in 1652 and stayed at Swarthmoor Hall, the home of Judge Fell and his wife Margaret. Margaret Fell became a Quaker and meetings were held in the hall from 1652 until the building of the meeting house, which was probably converted from an existing cottage and barn. It was in regular use from 1690.

It is, like most of the early meeting houses, a simple rectangular building without ornament. Originally it had casement windows, some of which survive, but those in the main room are modern. The porch leads to a narrow passage between screens which are moveable. To the left is the main room with a raised platform at the far end. This, and the present panelling, were installed about 1814. To the right the room above was used for women's meetings and, later, as a schoolroom.

Fox gave to the local Friends his ebony bed, a large elbow chair and a sea chest. The bed and chest are kept in Swarthmoor Hall, which is owned by the Society of Friends. The chair is in the meeting house.

Other early meeting houses in the locality and still in use are at Rookhow; Colthouse near Hawkshead; and Brigflatts near Sedbergh.

A Quartet of Chapels

They were anxious not to look like the church, which held them in contempt; nor like a house, for they were places of worship; nor like a theatre, for they were sacred piles.

John Betjeman, *First and Last Loves*

43

Hamsterley Baptist Chapel, County Durham
18th century

OS 88 NZ 115565. Hamsterley. On A694 between Newcastle and Consett

[C]

A Baptist congregation was established in Hexham (67,N) in 1652 by Thomas Tillam, who came from London in response to local requests for a minister. Within a short time other congregations were formed in the same area, meeting at first at the houses of members. In 1715 a chapel was built at Hamsterley, followed in 1717 by a chapel at Rowley, nearby.

The Hamsterley chapel was rebuilt in 1774 and although the adjacent Sunday School has been altered since, chapel and manse remain in their original simple but attractive form. The galleried interior of the chapel is still largely intact.

44

Newbiggin Methodist Chapel, County Durham
18th century and later

OS 92 NY 915276. Newbiggin. 2 miles (3.2km) NW of Middleton-in-Teesdale, on B6277 and minor road in village

[C]

The chapel was built in 1760 and is said to be the oldest Methodist chapel in continuous use since the days of John Wesley. Wesley visited the northern dales many times, typically preaching at

Hamsterley Baptist chapel. RCHME

Newbiggin Methodist chapel. C F STELL

9 a.m. in Weardale, at Newbiggin in Teesdale at noon, and then crossing to Swaledale to preach in the evening. He found a ready response among the isolated communities of farmers and lead miners and after initial meetings in local farmhouses the Newbiggin chapel was built to hold 200 people.

The present character of the chapel and the adjacent school owe much to a rebuilding of 1860 when the front of the chapel was altered and the building heightened. The interior also was reorganised but it retains a pulpit said to have been used by John Wesley and brought from a nearby farmhouse where some of the early meetings were held. Its simplicity is typical of those of its time.

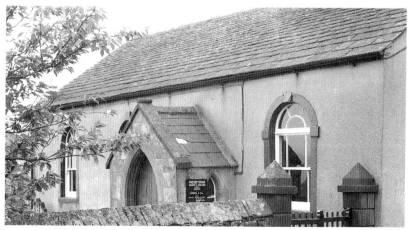

Penruddock Presbyterian chapel. C F STELL

Ravenstonedale Congregational chapel. RCHME

45

Penruddock Presbyterian Chapel, Cumbria
18th century and later

OS 90 NY 425275. Penruddock. 5 miles (8km) W of Penrith, on A66 and minor road
[C]

The present chapel dates from about 1789. It replaces an earlier building on the same site built before 1712 by Isaac Noble, son of John Noble, a yeoman farmer of Penruddock. In 1661 John Noble and others left the parish church of Greystoke (C) on the resignation of the Revd Richard Gilpin, whose puritan views forced him to leave the church, and formed an independent congregation, meeting in private houses in the area. John Noble died in 1705 and may have left money to build the chapel which a deed of 1712 refers to as 'newly erected'. The interior was entirely

refitted in 1864 and the porch added, but the rest of the chapel is as it was built in 1789, a simple, late-Georgian structure with round-headed windows, rendered walls and slated roof.

46

Ravenstonedale Congregational Chapel, Cumbria
18th century and later

OS 91 NY 723039. Ravenstonedale. 5 miles (8km) SW of Kirkby Stephen, on A685 and minor road
[C]

The 'High Chapel', as it is called, was built in 1726. Its origins, however, go back to 1662 when Christopher Jackson, newly ejected from the church at Crosby Garrett, began to hold meetings in houses in the Ravenstonedale area,

probably under the protection of Lord Wharton of Wharton Hall. In 1692, after the Act of Toleration, meetings at the house of George Parkin were licensed, followed by the building of the chapel some years later.

Nothing of the early interior survives. In 1868 new furnishings replaced the original three-decker pulpit and pews, and, on the outside, the present tall, round-headed windows were substituted for a double row of smaller windows. The present pulpit, reading desk and communion rails come from Cheshunt College, in memory of Bernard Manning, son of a minister of the chapel.

In 1838 the then minister and many of the congregation left to establish the Wesleyan chapel which is further down the village. Also of great interest in Ravenstonedale is the parish church which began as the church of a small Gilbertine monastery, whose remains are to be seen north of the church. The church was rebuilt in 1744 and has a remarkably fine Georgian interior.

5

Castles and Fortifications

No other part of England has such a splendid array of castles as the four northern counties. In number and in variety they are unequalled. Among the earliest are the earthwork and timber castles built by Norman lords in the years after the Conquest to hold and subdue their newly acquired lands and subjects. The best example, because it has escaped later alterations, is the motte and bailey castle at **Elsdon** (53,N), but the mottes of other Norman castles can be seen, overshadowed by later fortifications, at **Alnwick** (47,N), **Norham** (57,N), and **Warkworth** (60,N), and more prominently displayed at Durham (66,D).

In the 12th century many castles were fortified with stone walls, replacing the timber palisades of the earlier defences. This was the age, too, of the massive rectangular towers, or keeps, which are often the most memorable parts of medieval castles. They were both the residences of their lords and the most heavily defended buildings within the castle walls. Fine examples survive at Bowes (D), Brough (64,C), Prudhoe (N), and Newcastle upon Tyne (71,T), where the keep was built between 1172 and 1177 by Henry II and is one of the best of its type.

An alternative form of stronghold was the shell-keep, a walled enclosure usually built on top of the motte and with accommodation within the circuit of its walls. One was built at Alnwick in the 12th century and still remains at the centre of the castle, much altered in later times. Durham was given a shell-keep in the 14th century but this also has undergone much rebuilding.

Crusaders returning from the Holy Land brought new ideas of castle design which they put into practice in their English castles. So, during the 13th century, greater attention was paid to the outer circuit of walls, strengthening them with towers and building powerful gatehouses to guard their entrances. Warkworth is a good example of this new method of fortification, with both mural

towers and a new gatehouse, and at **Brougham** (50,C), Carlisle (65,C), Norham, Alnwick, Prudhoe (N), **Tynemouth** (59,T), and Newcastle, castle entrances were strengthened, either with new gatehouses or with barbicans placed in front of the gateways for additional protection. The best example, however, of this new type of fortification is **Dunstanburgh** (52,N). Here a curtain wall with towers surrounds the headland, and the gatehouse is a massive structure, the principal residence as well as the most heavily fortified part of this early 14th-century castle.

Elsewhere in England during the later Middle Ages the castle was in decline. By contrast, in the northern counties the threat from Scottish armies and raiding parties continued to make defence a necessity. The effect on smaller buildings is described in chapter 7. In larger strongholds, and especially those close to the border, defences were maintained and improved, and newly established castles, while paying more attention to domestic convenience, still kept a posture of defence.

Raby (58,D) was virtually rebuilt about 1378, and made into a formidable stronghold, and **Lumley** (55,D), dating from the late 14th century, is grim and uncompromising even with its 18th-century modifications. **Langley** (54,N) dates from about 1350 and Penrith (C) is a new castle of the late 14th century. Smaller, but still well fortified, are the castles at Dacre (C), Etal (N), and Bothal (N) dating from the 14th century, and also Hylton (T) built about 1400. At Warkworth the defences of this powerful castle were strengthened with a new keep, built in the early 15th century, which in its design and appearance is one of the most magnificent military buildings in England.

The increasing use of cannon in the 15th century brought new methods of defence. At Carlisle, Norham, and Tynemouth, changes were made to accommodate cannon and to withstand

Alnwick castle. The barbican. AFK

bombardment, but the finest example of the new system of defence is at **Berwick-upon-Tweed** (49,N) where the fortifications, started about 1555, are among the earliest examples of this type of fortification in northern Europe. The new defences replaced a medieval wall around the town, and it is appropriate here to mention the medieval town walls of Carlisle and Newcastle, still surviving in part, and Durham, of which little is now visible. Nor should one omit from this brief survey the defences built to protect monasteries and friaries such as Tynemouth especially, but also Lanercost (39,C), Lindisfarne (38,N), and Hulne (N); evidence that the fury of the Scots spared no-one and made fortification a necessity to the end of the 16th century.

A different enemy, the Dutch, caused the building of **Clifford's Fort** (51,T), a late 17th-century artillery fort at North Shields, at the mouth of the Tyne. The smaller fort on Holy Island, Osborne's Fort, was built in the same period, reinforcing the 16th battery on the cliffs above the island's harbour. The final chapter of fortification belongs to the 20th century. The fort at North Shields (T) was active as a submarine mining base in the 1914–18 war, and the gun batteries at Tynemouth were manned in both world wars.

47

Alnwick Castle, Northumberland
Middle Ages and later

OS 81 NU 187136. Alnwick.
On N side of town

[A]

Alnwick is both castle and stately home, the seat of the duke of Northumberland. It began as a motte and bailey castle and the mound or motte can still be seen in the centre of the enclosure, although now it carries a cluster of towers and buildings. In the 12th century a shell-keep was added to the motte and the two baileys were walled. In 1173 the castle was besieged by William the Lion, king of Scots, but not captured. It is not clear

Alnwick castle. RCHME

whether this was because of its strength or because a truce was arranged, but, evidently, it was too powerful to be easily overrun. In the following year the Scots returned but were defeated outside the town by an English army and William the Lion captured.

In 1309 the castle and barony of Alnwick were acquired by Henry de Percy, which marked the beginning of Percy ownership and the beginning, too, of a great strengthening of the castle which made it one of the chief border fortresses. The shell-keep was replaced by a circle of seven towers enclosing a small courtyard around which were the principal living quarters. Towers were added to the bailey walls and two powerful gatehouses were built, one separating the two baileys and the other, at the outer entrance, strengthened with a barbican and drawbridge. The figures on the parapets, here and elsewhere in the castle, are 18th-century but very probably replace medieval originals.

During the 16th and 17th centuries the castle was neglected and, by the time of the 1st duke of Northumberland (1750–86), parts were in ruins. Repairs were put in hand and the chambers inside the keep remodelled to the designs of Robert Adam in gothick style.

Two fireplaces survive from this work. The rest was swept away by a second restoration in the middle of the 19th century when the 4th duke called in Anthony Salvin to make appropriately 'medieval' additions to the exterior. For the interior a team of Italian craftsmen were employed to create a suite of state rooms with classical decoration. It is one of the most richly decorated Victorian interiors in England, enhanced by an outstanding collection of paintings and other works of art. In the Abbot's Tower, one of the towers on the bailey wall, is the regimental museum of the Royal Northumberland Fusiliers.

In the 18th century the park was landscaped by 'Capability' Brown and provided with columns, towers, and other ornaments to give appropriately picturesque points of interest. (See introduction to chapter 10.) In the grounds also is the gatehouse of a Premonstratensian abbey, and the remains of Hulne priory. The Lion Bridge and Denwick Bridge are by John Adam. Permits to walk in the park are obtainable from the Estate Office in the castle.

The town of Alnwick was walled and in Bondgate, at the south-east end of the town, stands the 15th-century Hotspur

Gate. In the centre of the town is the market-hall (Northumberland Hall) built at the expense of the 3rd duke in 1826, and nearby is the 18th-century town hall. St Michael's church, on the west side of the town, is mainly 15th-century but restored.

48

Bamburgh Castle, Northumberland
Middle Ages and later

OS 75 NU 184351. Bamburgh.
5 miles (8km) E of Belford on B1342

[A]

Bamburgh Castle has a superb site, its walls enclosing the top of a huge, precipitous rock next to the sea. The site was occupied in prehistoric times and in the 6th century was the principal fortress of the early kings of Bernicia. The Normans established a castle here which, in 1095, was besieged and taken by William II from the rebellious Robert Mowbray, earl of Northumberland. For a time in the 12th century it was under Scottish control, but from 1157 onwards it remained a royal castle, guarding the East March against the Scots. During the Wars of the Roses it was, like Dunstanburgh (52,N), held by the Lancastrians and twice came under siege, in 1462 and 1464. It was damaged by cannon fire and thereafter fell into ruin.

The castle is divided into three baileys with an entrance at the east end, defended by a gatehouse and barbican. The keep dates from the 12th century, but its interior was extensively altered in the 18th century when the castle was purchased by Lord Crewe, bishop of Durham, repaired, and made into school rooms, an infirmary, a granary, and accommodation for ship-wrecked sailors. At the end of the 19th century there was a second major restoration, by Lord Armstrong, owner of Cragside (87,N), who built the present great hall and chambers on the south side of the castle. The architect was C J Ferguson of Carlisle.

Parts of the castle are still lived in. Other rooms, including the state rooms, have a display of arms and armour, family portraits, china and furniture. There is also the Armstrong Museum of Industrial Archaeology, which has exhibits illustrating the life and work of Sir William, later Lord Armstrong, inventor, engineer and industrialist, who died in 1900. In the village is the Grace Darling Museum commemorating the heroic rescue in 1834 of the survivors from the *Forfarshire* near the Longstone lighthouse.

49

Berwick-upon-Tweed Fortifications, Northumberland
Middle Ages and 16th century

OS 75 NT 000530. Berwick-upon-Tweed. On N and E sides of town

[A] EH

Berwick stands on the north bank of the River Tweed, a frontier town whose possession was hotly disputed by Scots and English. It has both medieval and Elizabethan fortifications though more of the latter than the former. The medieval castle, in the north-west part of the town, was destroyed by the railway and Berwick station, and very little of the medieval town wall remains. There is a length on the high bank above the river in the north-west quarter, and also some of the Water Tower which protected the medieval quay.

The glory of Berwick, in a military sense, is the circuit of ramparts and bastions built in the 16th century to meet the threat of artillery. The system was developed in Italy and soon adopted elsewhere. The Berwick defences are the best example in Britain of this type of fortification and one of the earliest in northern Europe.

The first step in modernising the medieval defences was the construction of a circular tower (Lord's Mount) at the north-east angle, but this was little more than a traditional tower equipped with casemates for cannon. The new type of fortification was introduced first in the

Bamburgh castle. AEROFILMS

form of a citadel on the east side of the town, of which nothing remains, and then, starting in 1558 or early in 1559, the construction of the massive works which still survive on the north and east. The principal engineer was an Englishman, Sir Richard Lee, advised in the later stages of the work by two Italians, Giovanni Portinari and Jacopo Contio. The original intention was to build a complete circuit around the town, but by 1569, when work ceased, only two sides had been finished.

A tour of the fortifications should begin at Meg's Mount at the north-west corner. East of this is Scotsgate, rebuilt in the 19th century. Beyond the gate are Cumberland Bastion, in the middle of the north defences, and Brass Bastion at the north-east angle. South of Brass Bastion is Cow Port, the only unaltered

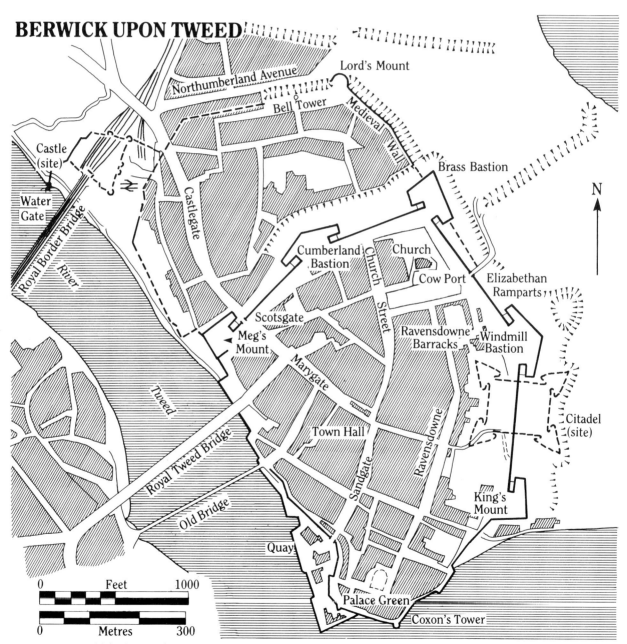

BERWICK UPON TWEED

Berwick-upon-Tweed (after I MacIvor). EH

16th-century gateway, and in the middle of the east defences, Windmill Bastion. At the south-east angle is King's Mount, the last of the five bastions.

Glimpses of the town can be obtained from the ramparts but its streets and buildings repay a closer look. It has a handsome 18th-century town hall, an 18th-century barracks, Ravensdowne Barracks, the earliest built in Britain, and, nearby, the church of Holy Trinity, built between 1650 and 1652. In the lower part of the town the Governor's House on Palace Green and the Custom House on Quay Walls are worth seeing, and there is a good view from Quay Walls of the Old Bridge, completed in 1634. Upstream are the Royal Tweed Bridge (1925–8) and, beyond, towering above the river, the Royal Border Bridge, Robert Stephenson's great railway crossing which was opened by Queen Victoria on 29 August 1850. The Berwick Museum and the Museum of the King's Own Scottish Border Regiment are housed in Ravensdowne Barracks, which also has a military exhibition (EH).

Fortifications between Cumberland and Brass Bastions, Berwick-upon-Tweed. JOHN BETHELL

50

Brougham Castle, Cumbria
12th century and later

OS 90 NY 537290. Brougham. 1½ miles (2.4km) SE of Penrith on A66

[A] EH

Bowes, Brough and Brougham castles are familiar landmarks for travellers on the A66 as it crosses the Pennines from Scotch Corner (A1) to Penrith (M6). For much of its route the modern carriageway follows the Roman road and all three castles are on or near Roman forts. At Brougham the earthworks of the Roman fort of Brocavum are just to the south of the castle, and there are Roman tombstones and altars, found locally, on display within the castle.

The oldest part of the castle is the 12th-century keep, originally entered at first floor level from a staircase on its east side. It has only one room on each floor and its topmost part is a 13th-century addition. North of the keep, and attached to it, is a formidable gatehouse

Brougham castle. RCHME

which is in two parts, divided by a small open area. Each part has a portcullis and gate at ground floor level and, above, a suite of chambers which is linked with those in the keep. Within the courtyard of the castle are the remains of the great hall, great chamber, kitchen and chapel, all at first floor level on the east and south sides of the courtyard, and on the

west side are the scanty foundations of a bakehouse and other domestic buildings.

The most remarkable owner of Brougham castle was Lady Anne Clifford, a lady of strong will and a great builder who restored the castle in 1651, lived in the chambers above the gatehouse, and died here in 1676. Her titles are recorded on a plaque in the outer gatehouse. She rebuilt the neighbouring churches of St Ninian (Ninekirk) north-east of the castle, and St Wilfrid near the remains of Brougham Hall to the south-west. As well as the work at Brougham, she restored her castles at Skipton, Appleby (61,C), Brough (64,C), and Pendragon (Mallerstang). Her tomb is at Appleby church together with that of her mother, Margaret, Countess of Cumberland. East of the castle, on an embankment by the side of the A66, is the Countess's Pillar (EH), a stone column with coats of arms and a sun dial, set up by Lady Anne in 1654 to mark the site of her last parting from her mother.

51
Clifford's Fort, Tyne and Wear
17th century and later

OS 88 NZ 363685. North Shields. On the coast 8 miles (12.8km) E of Newcastle. Site is on quayside
[C]

Clifford's Fort was built in 1672 as a consequence of the successful Dutch raid on the River Medway in Kent five years earlier. To avoid a repetition, coastal defences were strengthened and as part of this programme a new fort was constructed to guard the mouth of the Tyne. By this time the defences of Tynemouth Castle were obsolete and improvements such as the 16th-century battery to the south of the castle and a 'little fort' of 1642, built to deter the Scots, were considered insufficient.

The new fort was designed by Martin Beckman, a Swedish military engineer in the service of the Crown and shortly to be appointed Chief Engineer. It has an irregular shape with its long axis north-south and a gateway in its north wall. It was also built on two levels. On the lower level facing the river on its east, south-east, and south sides, was a powerful battery of guns mounted on a platform behind a low wall. Behind this was the main body of the fort at a higher

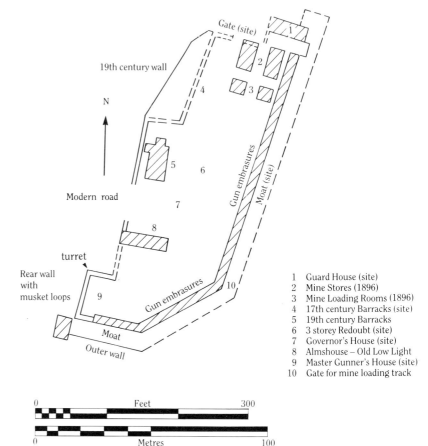

1 Guard House (site)
2 Mine Stores (1896)
3 Mine Loading Rooms (1896)
4 17th century Barracks (site)
5 19th century Barracks
6 3 storey Redoubt (site)
7 Governor's House (site)
8 Almshouse – Old Low Light
9 Master Gunner's House (site)
10 Gate for mine loading track

Clifford's Fort, North Shields (after Society of Antiquaries, Newcastle). EH

level, protected towards the rear by a high wall with corner turrets and musket loops. Within the fort was a three-storey redoubt containing powder magazines and stores on the ground floor and living quarters for the garrison above.

During the 18th century the defences were improved and more military accommodation provided. On the river sides the front wall was raised, the interior levelled, and embrasures formed for the guns. A ditch was dug in front. Within the fort a Governor's House, a Master Gunner's House and a new barrack block were built, and outside the fort on higher ground a new fortified barrack was established to give additional landward protection.

The fort was manned and kept in a state of readiness through the

Napoleonic wars and into the 19th century, but improvements in artillery were reducing its effectiveness and, ironically, increasing the importance of Tynemouth Castle as a military base. In 1888 the fort was made the headquarters of a submarine mining and signalling corps. Some of the older buildings, including the 17th-century redoubt, were demolished and new stores and workshops built. It was slightly increased in size and a new gateway made in the south-east wall to enable a narrow gauge track to take mines from the fort to the quayside. The fort was used in both world wars but between the wars it was purchased by Tynemouth Corporation. After 1945 it was put to commercial use, its walls neglected and many of its military buildings demolished.

Much has been lost but with a knowledge of its lay-out and some tenacity it is possible to trace the remains of the fort walls and also the mine stores, now converted into fish curing houses. There is also a former almshouse on the site of an 18th-century lighthouse, and a 19th-century block of soldiers' quarters, now offices. It is a rare and important survival, the best example of its type north of the Thames, and recent conservation work is a heartening sign that its historical value is being increasingly appreciated.

52

Dunstanburgh Castle, Northumberland
Late Middle Ages

OS 75 NU 258220. 8 miles (12.8km) NE of Alnwick on B1340 and minor roads to Craster or Dunstan Steads near Embleton, then by footpaths

[A] EH

The site of the castle is wonderfully dramatic. It stands on a rocky promontory jutting out into the North Sea with high cliffs on the north side and steep slopes to the west. Although the 'burgh' part of the name suggests an Anglian fortified settlement, the only visible remains are those of the medieval castle begun by Thomas, 2nd earl of Lancaster in 1313. Earl Thomas surrounded the headland with a strong wall and built a massive gatehouse on the south side where the castle was most vulnerable. He also began work on a huge ditch to the south and west and made a port below the castle wall at the south-east corner. This is now an area of marsh cut off by a dyke and wall but, originally, it was open to the sea and capable of being used by the small boats of the time.

Alterations were made by John of Gaunt, duke of Lancaster, later in the 14th century. The gatehouse passage was blocked and a new gateway with a barbican made to one side. Behind the gatehouse a new wall and tower were built for extra defence. The purpose was to make the gatehouse and its accommodation impregnable, a secure base for its owner who in 1380 was appointed lieutenant in the Marches towards Scotland. Its defences were tested and proved in 1385 when a Scottish attack was beaten off.

During the Wars of the Roses Dunstanburgh was a Lancastrian stronghold. It was besieged in 1462, and again in 1464 when it was taken by the forces of Edward IV. Thereafter it was little used and fell into ruin. In 1604 it was sold by the Crown to a private owner.

The area enclosed by the walls is 11 acres (4.5ha). It is a huge space, bare and windswept, and its present appearance is rather misleading. Missing from the scene are the timber buildings and shelters which housed the servants, stores, horses and livestock needed to maintain the castle and its garrison. During military campaigns it was filled with troops and supplies, many brought in by sea through its port. The only reminder of these additional buildings is an enclosure against the east curtain where there was once a great barn.

53

Elsdon Castle, Northumberland
Early Middle Ages

OS 80 NY 937935. Elsdon. 12 miles (19km) SW of Rothbury on B6341, or by A696 from Newcastle

[D]

Motte and bailey castles were the most common form of fortification used by the Normans after the Conquest to establish themselves in their newly-won territory. They were quick and simple to build, using earth and timber and forced labour, and very effective against attack. Their usual form was a high mound or motte surrounded by a ditch and with a wooden tower and stockade on top. At the foot of the mound was an enclosure or bailey which contained the living quarters of the lord and household, and accommodation for his retainers. The bailey also was defended by a stockade and ditch.

Elsdon is an excellent example of this type of castle, its earthworks largely intact and unaffected by later masonry walls and buildings. The motte has a ditch on the east and north, but on the

Dunstanburgh castle. EH

Elsdon castle. MUSEUM OF ANTIQUITIES OF NEWCASTLE UPON TYNE

west and south the natural steepness of the ground made a ditch here unnecessary. Similarly, the bailey has a rampart and ditch on the east and north, also on the side facing the motte, but not on the west. It was built by the Umfravilles probably soon after the Conquest and held until the mid-12th century when it was abandoned in favour of Harbottle Castle, 8 miles (12.75km) to the north.

The village is attractive and to the north of St Cuthbert's church is a 14th-century vicar's pele, similar to the one at Corbridge (77,N). At Elsdon it is still occupied.

54

Langley Castle,
Northumberland
Late Middle Ages

OS 87 NY 835625. Haydon Bridge. 1½ miles (2.4km) SW of Haydon Bridge on A686
[C]

Langley Castle was built about the year 1350 by Sir Thomas de Lucy. He inherited the property in 1343, fought at the battles of Crecy and Neville's Cross in 1346, and had completed his stronghold by 1365 when it is referred to as the 'castle and manor of Langley'. Later it passed to the Umfravilles and, in 1381, by marriage to Henry Percy, 1st earl of Northumberland.

It belongs to the period of castle buildings that in Northumberland produced Chillingham and Ford, and in County Durham, Lumley (55), Brancepeth and Raby (58). But whereas these are great courtyard castles, Langley is tall and compact. In plan it is oblong with four large corner towers. The central block has one large chamber on each of its four floors with the great hall at first floor level and the great chamber above. The towers, which rise a stage higher, contain subsidiary chambers, except for the south-west tower which has a battery of eight garderobes (latrines) emptying at the base of the tower into a pit which, apparently, could be flushed by diverting a nearby stream. Entrance to the castle was on the east side at ground level. The doorway is protected by a portcullis and leads to a stone newel staircase which gives access to the great hall above. The south entrance is modern.

The castle was in ruins by 1541 and remained so until the end of the 19th century when it was thoroughly restored. Many of the windows were renewed and also the battlements and higher walls. Little of the medieval interior remains, but externally it is remarkably impressive; a huge, uncompromising building, formidable in appearance and well equipped for defence. It is presently used as a hotel.

55

Lumley Castle,
County Durham
Late Middle Ages

OS 88 NZ 288511. Chester-le-Street. 1 mile (1.6km) E of Chester-le-Street on B1284
[C]

Lumley Castle was built by Sir Ralph Lumley about 1389. He was granted a license to crenellate by the bishop of Durham in that year, and by the king in 1392. It is built with four ranges surrounding an internal courtyard and has massive towers at each corner, a plan adopted in the 14th century by several northern lords seeking palatial accommodation combined with a measure of defence. Raby Castle (58) in the same county is another of this type, though less regular, and, in Northumberland, Chillingham and Ford also belong to this group. The best example, and the least altered, is Bolton Castle in Wensleydale, North Yorkshire.

The gatehouse is in the east range with the great hall across the courtyard on the opposite side. It is at first floor level and has an entrance marked with a display of heraldry, the work of John, Lord Lumley, in the 16th century, who also installed the Tudor windows. More alterations were made in the early 18th century when Sir John Vanbrugh provided what he described in a letter as 'a General Design for the whole, which consists in altering the House both for State, Beauty and Convenience.' The outer fronts of the hall range and the

Langley castle. AFK

south range were given classical facades, and a new corridor and staircase made on the south side of the courtyard, but the only interior bearing Vanbrugh's imprint is a vaulted chamber in the south-west tower which has rusticated stone pillars, deeply incised. Despite its Tudor and Georgian alterations Lumley is still essentially a medieval stronghold whose owner built for strength and security as well as for comfort and magnificence. In recent years the castle was used as a hall of residence by Durham University, and latterly as a hotel.

56

Naworth Castle, Cumbria
Middle Ages and later

OS 86 NY 560626. Brampton.
2 miles (3.2km) NE of Brampton
on A69 and minor road

[A]

Ralph, Lord Dacre, was granted a license to fortify his house at Naworth in 1335. It was a well chosen site. The ground falls away steeply on three sides, and on the fourth, towards the south, Dacre built two powerful towers with a wall between and a gatehouse in front. There was also, probably, a ditch, but this has been smoothed away by later landscaping. The other three sides were fortified with walls and, probably, towers, forming a courtyard around which were the domestic buildings, the hall on the east side, and the principal chambers and chapel on the south.

Later changes have been extensive. The castle was remodelled in the early-16th century by Thomas, Lord Dacre of Gillesland, who fought at the battle of Flodden in 1513 and whose tomb is in Lanercost Priory (39,C). Further work was done in the early 17th century by Lord William Howard who obtained Naworth through marriage with Elizabeth Dacre. After a fire in 1844 repairs were supervised by Anthony Salvin for the 6th earl of Carlisle.

The principal interiors are the great hall in the east range, unusually long and with a fine timber roof by Salvin,

Lumley castle. RCHME

Naworth castle. AEROFILMS

and the library, formerly the chapel, which has a panel depicting the battle of Flodden, designed by Burne-Jones. George James Howard, 9th earl of Carlisle, an artist himself, was a friend of Edward Burne-Jones and William Morris and supported their work. Stained glass by Morris and Burne-Jones can be seen in the windows of St Martin's church, Brampton, built in 1874–8 to the design of Philip Webb.

57

Norham Castle, Northumberland
12th century and later

OS 75 NT 907476. Norham. 7 miles (11km) SW of Berwick on A698 and B6470, and minor road off B6470

[A] EH

Norham Castle stands on the south bank of the River Tweed, commanding a crossing of the river. Together with the castles of Berwick (49,N) and Wark-upon-Tweed (N) it protected the eastern part of the border against the Scots and bore the brunt of many Scottish attacks. It belonged to the bishops of Durham

Raby castle. RCHME

Norham castle. EH

who also owned the surrounding territory of Norhamshire which was separate from the county of Northumberland. The first castle was established here in 1121, a motte and bailey castle of which the earthworks partially survive. It was taken by the Scots in 1136 and again in 1138 when its defences were destroyed, and rebuilt thirty years later with stone fortifications. The lower part of the keep and parts of the inner and outer walls of the castle date from this time.

Besieged many times but rarely taken, the defences were improved and strengthened over the next 300 years. However, in 1531 its outer walls were battered down by Scottish artillery, which included the huge cannon 'Mons Meg' now on display at Edinburgh Castle. Less than two weeks after the Scots had taken Norham they were defeated at Flodden Field, 5 miles (8km) south-west of Norham, near Branxton village. The castle was rebuilt, with remodelled defences, and with its own artillery. Port holes for cannon are still to be seen in its walls. In Elizabeth's reign maintenance was neglected and the castle fell into disuse and ruin. Later, in picturesque decline, it attracted writers and painters. Turner visited it in 1797 and made the castle the subject of several paintings over a period of forty years; Sir Walter Scott used the

castle as the setting for the opening scenes of his epic poem *Marmion*, written in 1808.

The massive keep is the dominant part of the castle, but the remaining defences, though ruinous, are worth study, especially the defensive arrangements of the two gatehouses and the 16th-century provision for artillery. The great hall and other domestic quarters were in the inner ward.

Norham village developed under the protection of the castle. It has a fine church (St Cuthbert's), with a 12th-century chancel and south arcade.

58

Raby Castle, County Durham
Middle Ages and later

OS 92 NZ 129218. Staindrop. 7 miles (11km) NE of Barnard Castle on A688

[A]

When viewed across the park Raby looks a 19th-century castle, more a mansion in gothic dress than a building capable of serious defence. It is true that much was done to it in the 18th and 19th centuries, and the removal of the outer wall and filling in of the moat have especially altered its external appearance. Nevertheless, most of the building is 14th-century, built about 1378 for John, Lord Nevill, and more formidable than may first appear.

It is a quadrangular castle, its towers and side ranges enclosing a central courtyard. It is not strictly regular like its contemporary, Bolton Castle in North Yorkshire, but, like Bolton and Sheriff Hutton, a Nevill castle in Yorkshire built about 1382, its strength lies in four powerful towers, rising above the lower ranges of buildings which close the circuit and complete its defence.

Entry to the courtyard is through a vaulted gateway in the west range. In front, at first floor level, is the great hall, lengthened and entirely remodelled internally in the 19th century. To its left is the kitchen. This occupies the whole of a tower, rises through two storeys to a vaulted roof with central lantern, and is one of the finest medieval kitchens in the country, barely altered save for a few items of 19th-century and modern cooking equipment. The rest of the interior on show to visitors is largely of the 18th and 19th centuries. The entrance hall, re-named the Baron's Hall, is mostly the work of William Burn who, in the 19th century, also designed

the Octagon Drawing-Room with its elaborate woodwork and ceiling. The chapel is on the site of the medieval chapel but at a different level and now with 19th-century decoration and fittings. Most of the rooms are contained within the fabric of the 14th-century castle, proof that, when built, the castle was intended to provide its owner with both security and accommodation on a princely scale. Tombs and effigies of the owners of Raby are in St Mary's church, Staindrop, which is well worth a visit, as is the village with its large green and handsome 18th and 19th century buildings.

59
Tynemouth Castle and Priory, Tyne and Wear
Middle Ages and later

OS 88 NZ 374694. Tynemouth. 9 miles (14.5km) E of Newcastle on A193

[A] EH

Castle and priory occupy a rocky headland on the north side of the Tyne, well defended by cliffs to the north and

east and by steep slopes to the river on the south. For centuries it has been a stronghold and a centre of religious life.

There is evidence of prehistoric settlement but no proof, as yet, of Roman use. In the 7th century a monastery was established on the headland which became a focus of pilgrimage as the burial place of St Oswin, king of Deira, but in 865 it was destroyed by the Danes and finally abandoned in 1008. After the Conquest the ancient church of the monastery was repaired, but there is now no trace of this early building.

The present castle and priory owe their origins to Robert de Mowbray, Norman earl of Northumberland, and, from its foundation, the Benedictine priory has sheltered within the castle's defences and occupied much of its inner area. The gatehouse at the entrance is the most formidable part of the surviving defences but parts remain of the circuit of walls, the best length being in the south-west corner. Flanking the gatehouse are 16th-century fortifications designed, as at Berwick (49,N), to withstand artillery.

The priory was founded in 1090 with monks from the abbey of St Albans in Hertfordshire. Parts of the nave and transepts of the present church date from the first phase of building and there is other early work in the living-quarters of the monks south of the church, but the most memorable part of the ruined building is the soaring east end, begun about 1190 and happily spared the general destruction after closure of the priory in 1539. The nave was retained for use as a parish church until the 17th century, but this also is now ruinous. The only roofed building is the small Percy Chantry at the east end. Built in the 15th century it has an elaborate stone vault with huge bosses, carved with the figure of Christ, also saints, religious symbols, and heraldry of the Percy family.

The castle continued in use after the destruction of the priory and there was a military presence here into modern times. On the east cliff are gun emplacements of the 1914–18 war and in one of the magazines a small exhibition explains their use and history.

Tynemouth castle and priory. AEROFILMS

60

Warkworth Castle, Northumberland
12th century and later

OS 81 NU 247058. Warkworth.
7 miles (11km) SE of Alnwick
on A1068

[A] EH

Warkworth began as a motte and bailey castle exploiting a naturally strong position in a loop of the River Coquet. In the first half of the 12th century it was in the possession of Scottish earls of Northumberland who may have begun to rebuilt the castle in stone, but most of the curtain wall, its turrets and formidable gatehouse are the work of the de Claverings who held the castle from 1157 to 1332. On the death of the last of the family, Warkworth was granted by Edward III to Henry Percy,

lord of Alnwick, and for a time it became the favourite residence of the Percys, later earls of Northumberland.

Warkworth resisted two determined sieges by the Scots in 1327, but in 1405 it fell to the cannon of Henry IV's army during the crushing of a rebellion by the 1st earl. Northumberland's rebellion figures prominently in Shakespeare's *King Henry the Fourth*.

In the early 15th century, during the ownership of the first two Percy earls, the castle was transformed. The great hall was enlarged, a new and unusually large church was built across the bailey, and, on the motte, an older building was replaced by a new keep, a superb building elegant in appearance and ingenious in its planning. It is also remarkably complete so that, exceptionally, one can walk through the intricate web of rooms – hall, chambers, chapel, kitchens and cellars – built for a rich and powerful lord. The Percy lion, carved in stone, is on the north side of the keep.

The keep continued in use until the later part of the 16th century although the rest of the castle was neglected and parts demolished. The castle was damaged during the Civil War, and later pillaged for building materials, but the keep was repaired by the 4th duke of Northumberland in 1853–8, employing Anthony Salvin as his architect.

Warkworth village, a new borough established in the 12th century, stretches downhill from the castle to the bridge over the Coquet. The bridge is defended by a gatehouse and is one of the few fortified bridges in Britain. The shape of the village is still medieval with burgage plots flanking the street, but the present houses are mainly 18th and 19th-century. St Lawrence's church has a fine 12th-century vaulted chancel. Upstream from the castle is Warkworth Hermitage (EH), cut from the solid rock and containing a 14th-century chapel and several living rooms. Access is by boat, at weekends during the summer only.

Warkworth castle. AEROFILMS

6

Cities, Towns and Villages

Carlisle and Newcastle are cities with Roman origins. **Carlisle** (65,C) has under its streets the Roman town of Luguvalium, and part of **Newcastle** (71,T), in fact its castle, is built on the site of a Roman fort. But there was no continuity of use. The street pattern of Carlisle bears no relationship to the regular planning of its Roman predecessor, and the Roman fort at Newcastle was abandoned long before its burial under the Norman fortifications. Withdrawal of Roman rule in northern Britain saw the decay of its towns and the destruction of all forms of urban life.

In the centuries that followed England became a land of villages; in many areas, but not universally, of farms and dwellings surrounded by a pattern of open fields. The open fields have disappeared but the pattern of villages remains, especially in the North, in the main areas of Anglian settlement, that is to say east of the Pennines and, in Cumbria, in the vale of Eden and the valleys of the Kent and Lune. In the mountains, homesteads were small and scattered and villages rare.

Conquest by the Normans and their seizure of land imposed a new layer of settlement as well as a different form of control. They ruled through castles, sometimes placed in or near older settlements, often on new sites chosen for their strategic value. Castles became the centres of administration, of justice and of trade. Outside their gates communities sprang up, and, granted the privileges of holding markets and fairs, became the new towns of the region, small at first but, where conditions were favourable, growing through trade into substantial market towns.

At **Barnard Castle** (62,D) castle and town were established on a new site, close to a Roman crossing of the River Tees but not previously defended. Its settlement developed outside its gate with the market place immediately beyond the castle moat. **Appleby** (61,C), by contrast, was grafted on to an older

settlement, but the newer part, next to the castle and with a market, became the focus of the community. Some grew haphazardly, others were carefully planned with house plots, church, and market-place marked out in an orderly and deliberate design. One can still see this at Appleby and also at Warkworth (60,N) where, although the buildings have changed, the present community still lives within the boundary, and with the same ordered arrangement, of the medieval borough.

Newcastle developed under the protection of its castle, and the extent of the medieval town may still be traced along its impressive walls, surviving tenaciously within the modern city. Carlisle sprang from the castle established by William II, and its street plan together with the remains of the town wall mark the extent of the medieval borough. In Northumberland, Berwick (49), Alnwick (47) and Morpeth owe their existence to castles. In Cumbria the towns of Brampton, Egremont, and **Kendal** (68) also have their origins in castles.

The mere presence of a castle did not guarantee a thriving community. None developed at Brougham (50,C), at Bewcastle (23,C), or at Dunstanburgh (52,N). At Bowes (D), Bamburgh (48,N) and at **Brough** (64,C) their respective settlements never rose to more than village status, the one at Brough undermined by a more prosperous community on the Stainmore road where traders and merchants preferred the booths and stalls of Market Brough to the deliberately contrived and less convenient market by the castle. Nor were castles the only promoters of settlement. Abbeys and priories, although some sought seclusion, stimulated trade and brought new communities to their gates. At **Hexham** (67,N) the market-place of the town is next to the abbey church, decently separated from the monastic enclosure in the Middle Ages by a precinct wall, and at Cartmel (35,C) the little town still

The town hall, Berwick-upon-Tweed. AFK

clusters around the priory church.

At **Durham** (66,D) there is both abbey and castle, the stronghold of the prince-bishop. The town grew up below the castle walls, and its ancient bridges, streets and market-place still reflect its medieval origins. However, compared with its sister cities of Carlisle and Newcastle, it has remained modest in size, by-passed by commerce and industry and only spreading substantially over the surrounding hills in recent years.

Villages, too, suffered different fates. Many died, succumbing to famine and pestilence, to changes in land ownership, or to changes in agriculture, especially the drift in the later Middle Ages and in the 16th century from plough to pasture. The majority of deserted villages, like **Ogle** (72,N), occur in the eastern parts of Northumberland and County Durham, with a few in the lower valley of the Eden.

In more recent times villages have been removed deliberately and rebuilt on different sites at the behest of Georgian landowners wishing to beautify the surroundings of their new mansions, and perhaps to improve the accommodation of their tenants. So at Cambo near Wallington (96,N), Sir Walter Calverley Blackett laid out a new village about the year 1740, and at Belsay (86,N) in the 1830s Sir Charles Monck built a new village outside his gates. More ambitious than either of these were the new villages built on the Lowther estate south of Penrith. **Lowther** Newtown (70,C) was built by Sir John Lowther in the 1680s, followed by Lowther village, a larger, more ambitious scheme designed for Sir James Lowther by the architect Robert Adam. It was started about 1765 and, regrettably, never finished.

The effect of industry has been widespread and, in places, overwhelming. It led to the creation of the new town of Whitehaven (106,C) by the Lowther family whose fortunes came from the local coal-mines and from the trade of the port. At **Blanchland** (63,N) it led to the building of the squares and terraces within the remains of the abbey as housing for workers in the local lead-mines. It transformed the

coalfields, bringing new villages as well as new industry, just as, earlier, it had brought to southern Lakeland workers' cottages and the grander houses of iron-masters whose blast-furnaces revolutionised the making of iron (100,C). Industry transformed Newcastle and the whole of the lower Tyne. It turned the small medieval towns of Sunderland (T) and Darlington (D) into industrial giants. At Barrow-in-Furness (C) it created a 19th-century new town whose wide, tree-lined streets and regular lay-out are still distinguishable between the industrial quarter and the later suburbs. Today, there are the new towns of Washington (T), Peterlee (D) and Newton Aycliffe (D), the 20th-century response to communal needs.

61

Appleby, Cumbria
Middle Ages and later

OS 91 NY 683205. On A66 13 miles (21km) SE of Penrith

Before 1974, when the new county of Cumbria was created, Appleby was the county town of Westmorland and its preferred name is 'Appleby in Westmorland'. The earliest settlement was in Bongate, on the east side of the River Eden, around, but pre-dating, St Michael's church. The suffix '-by' in Appleby suggests a 10th-century settlement and a hog-back tombstone built into the north wall of the church, above a doorway, is evidence of a church

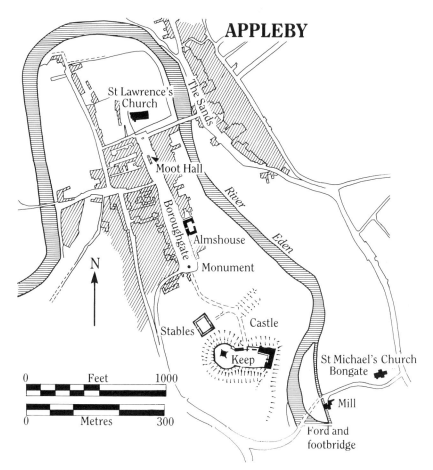

Appleby (after Millward and Robinson). EH

Boroughgate, Appleby. AFK

62

Barnard Castle, County Durham
Middle Ages and later

OS 92 NZ 050165. A66 from Scotch Corner or Penrith, or A67 from Darlington

[A] EH (Castle and Egglestone Abbey)

The town owes its existence to the castle founded here by Guy de Baliol in the 11th century, and takes its name from his nephew, Bernard de Baliol, who greatly enlarged the castle and, about 1155, granted the town its first charter. The castle is best seen from the southern bank of the river. From the town it is now entirely hidden from view and their relationship is difficult to appreciate.

The earliest settlement spread along the level ground to the east of the castle and its market-place was on the edge of the moat. Galgate was also an area of early settlement, on the line of a Roman road which forded the river upstream from the present bridge. At the south end of the market-place is the parish church of St Mary; Norman in origin but extended in the later Middle Ages and heavily restored in the 19th century.

Beyond the church, the town expanded down a steep hill called The Bank into Thorngate, and also east along Newgate. This pattern is still preserved, but in 1630 the castle was abandoned and partly destroyed, its moat filled in and a line of houses built along the western side of the market-place and down the western side of The Bank, entirely separating the castle from the town. The castle fell further into ruin and its grounds were used as gardens and pasture. It is now in the care of English Heritage.

Blagrove's House on The Bank survives from the late 16th century, but most of the buildings in the town centre are 18th-century and later, with Georgian houses surviving in Thorngate, Newgate, and at the bottom end of The Bank. In the 18th century the town prospered and woollen mills were established on the banks of the river.

here before AD 1000. The open fields of the village were probably to the north of Bongate, in the area near the railway station. St Michael's church, no longer in ecclesiastical use, has a 19th-century tower but the body of the church is medieval. It was repaired in the 17th century by Lady Anne Clifford.

Appleby castle, across the river, was built at the end of the 11th century by Ranulf de Meschines. It began as an earthwork castle which, later, was strengthened with stone walls and a massive 12th-century keep. For most of the Middles Ages it was in the ownership of Viponts and Cliffords. In the 17th century it was inherited by Lady Anne Clifford who repaired it and used it as one of her houses; the internal arrangements of the keep are largely her work. Opposite the keep is a fine late-17th-century house built by her son-in-law, the earl of Thanet. It is a private house and not open to the public, but the keep and the grounds, which are managed as a centre of the Rare Breeds Survival Trust, can be visited.

Below the castle a new town was established with a typical arrangement of burgage plots flanking the main street, Boroughgate. At its bottom end,

was a market-place and new church. The present buildings are mainly 18th-century and 19th-century but rebuilding has not changed the medieval pattern nor, mercifully, has modern development spoiled its very attractive character. The oldest building is the Moot Hall of 1596, re-windowed in the 18th century. At the top of the hill, on the east side, is St Anne's Hospital, an almshouse endowed by Lady Anne Clifford for thirteen women pensioners and built in 1651. The column outside the castle gates is also 17th-century.

St Lawrence's church, at the bottom of Boroughgate, has Norman masonry at the base of the tower, but most of the church is late medieval, with contributions from Lady Anne Clifford. She was buried here in 1676 and her tomb is in the north aisle with an ostentatious display of heraldry. The tomb of her mother, Margaret, countess of Cumberland, is nearby. The 17th-century organ is one of the earliest surviving organs in England. It was brought here from Carlisle cathedral in 1684. The attractive arcade and pavilions at the entrance to the churchyard were designed by Sir Robert Smirke and built in 1811.

Butter Market, Barnard Castle. RCHME

The handsome octagonal building at the south end of the market-place was built in 1747 to act as a covered market. It also served as the town lock-up, and on the upper floor as the town's council chamber. The bridge across the Tees was built in 1597 though its parapets, frequently damaged by oversized vehicles, are 18th-century, renewed after a flood.

In the outskirts of the town, along Newgate, is the Bowes Museum, built as a private house in 1869 by John Bowes, son of the earl of Strathmore. His architect was Jules Pellechet and its style is that of a French chateau. Its magnificent collection of furniture and paintings, now in the care of Durham County Council, was gathered by John Bowes and his wife, Josephine Benoîte, and first opened to the public in 1892 while the house was still privately owned. It is an astonishing building and a remarkable museum.

To the south-east, on the south bank of the Tees, are the ruins of Egglestone Abbey, founded in the 12th century by Ralph de Multon for a community of Premonstratensian canons. Its abbot and first canons came from Easby Abbey near Richmond in North Yorkshire.

63

Blanchland, Northumberland
Middle Ages and later

OS 87 NY 966504. 10 miles (16km) S of Hexham on B6306

Much of the village was built in the 18th century by the Lord Crewe Estate to

house miners working in local lead-mines, but its origins are older. On the north side of the square is the medieval gatehouse of Blanchland Abbey, and the square itself is the abbey's outer court. On the east side, the Lord Crewe hotel stands on the site of the abbey's west range and has medieval masonry within its walls. The garden of the hotel occupies the monastic cloister.

The abbey was founded in 1165 by Walter de Bolbec as a house of Premonstratensian canons. The site, like that of Shap abbey in Cumbria, was in a remote valley, here the Derwent, surrounded by wild moors. The abbey exploited local resources, establishing sheep-runs, a fulling mill, a corn mill and a silver refinery, and a village developed outside its gates. When the abbey was closed in 1539 the property was bought by the Radcliffes, later earls of Derwentwater, and in the early 17th century by Forsters of Bamburgh who made a house in the west range, now the hotel. Other buildings were made into cottages. The acquisition by the Lord Crewe Estate in 1752 led to further expansion and to the building of new houses for lead miners.

Most of the abbey church has been destroyed but its chancel and north transept, which has a tower at its north end, survive and are used as the parish church. Two small figures of Premonstratensian canons are to be

Abbey gatehouse, Blanchland. RCHME

found in the stained glass of the chancel windows, and there are three grave slabs, the most interesting of them commemorating Robert de Eglyston, the abbey huntsman.

64

Brough, Cumbria
Middle Ages and later

OS 91 NY 794141 and NY 795146.
On A66 between Bowes and Appleby

Brough castle and Appleby castle (61,C) were founded about the same time. They followed William Rufus's conquest of Cumbria in 1092 and were built to control the Eden valley and to defend it against the Scots. Brough, in upper Eden, also supervised the western end of the Stainmore Pass, and the road south into Lunesdale. At Brough the castle was established in the northern part of the Roman fort of Verterae, on a bluff above Swindale Beck, a tributary of the Eden. Its most prominent building is the 12th-century keep, but under the keep are earlier walls belonging to an 11th-century castle, and early masonry is to be seen in both the north and south curtain walls. The hall and other domestic buildings in the south-east quarter date from the 13th and 14th centuries, but are on the site of Norman structures and were themselves restored and altered by Lady Anne Clifford in the 17th century. She also restored the keep.

At Brough, as at Appleby, a new town grew up under the protection of the castle. To the east is the market-place which until recently was by the side of the road from Market Brough to Kirkby Stephen (C), now moved and re-made further to the east. On the north side of the market-place, behind the present houses, are the burgage plots of the early settlements and to the south, a short distance away, is the parish church of St Michael. Much of the church dates from the later Middle Ages and the tower from 1513, but it is a Norman foundation as may be seen from its masonry and especially its fine south doorway.

But whereas at Appleby the new town

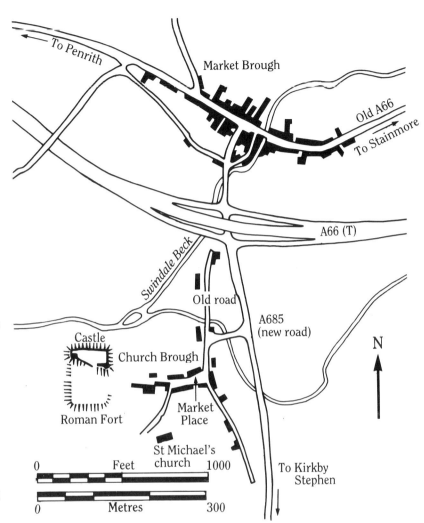

Church Brough and Market Brough (after Millward and Robinson). EH

Market Brough. BARRY STACEY/LIGHTWORK

thrived, at Brough it languished. The reason was the growth of a rival settlement half a mile (0.8km) to the north. It was established before the end of the 12th century astride the medieval highway from Stainmore to Penrith and Carlisle, serving the traffic along the route and benefitting from its trade. Now known as Market Brough, in 1197 it was referred to as Lower Brough to distinguish it from Upper Brough near the castle and church. Its fair, mentioned in 1314 and still held, later became one of the great centres of the northern cattle trade, and its market was established by charter in 1330. Its wide principal street, rising and curving to the east, is evidence of an extensive street-market, supplemented by a smaller market, now obscured by later buildings, at the road junction in the centre of the village.

None of the settlement's medieval buildings survive, but signs of its later prosperity can be seen in the substantial properties which line its main streets. They date from the 17th century onwards and include a late-Georgian inn at the centre, near the clock tower. Behind several of the buildings are yards formerly containing stables and warehouses. In the 19th century it was by-passed by the railway, and, more recently, its principal artery, the A66, was re-routed to the south, skirting the village and emptying its streets.

65

Carlisle, Cumbria

OS 85 NY 4055
[A] EH (Castle)

Carlisle stands on the site of the Roman town of Luguvalium. It was the principal Roman town of the area, the supply base for the western half of Hadrian's Wall, and a flourishing urban community with a water supply, sewers, and houses furnished with hypocausts. Excavations have provided tantalising glimpses of the buildings and also of a Roman fort near the castle, but all that can now be seen are Roman foundations in the grounds of the museum and the finds from

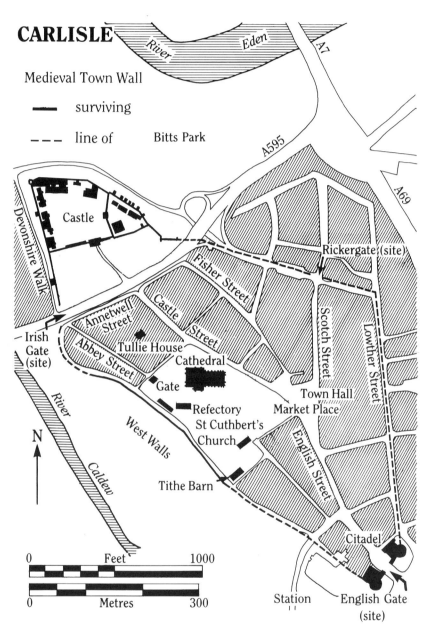

Carlisle (after RAI). EH

excavations which are on display in the museum itself.

After the departure of the Romans some form of urban life continued and in AD 685 Cuthbert, bishop of Lindisfarne, ordained priests at Carlisle and was shown the Roman walls and a fountain. However, apart from this brief

episode little is known about Carlisle in the turbulent centuries before the Norman Conquest. In 1066 it was part of the territory of the Scots and remained so until William II ('Rufus') conquered the area in 1092 and brought 'Caerlluel' and the whole of Cumbria under Norman rule. William built a castle at

Carlisle and except for a brief period during the reign of Stephen, and momentarily in 1745, it has remained in English hands, a stronghold against the Scots and the guardian of the western routes into England.

The Castle occupies a sandstone bluff on the north side of the city between the River Eden and the River Caldew. Its first defences were probably of earth and timber, but in the 12th century it was rebuilt in stone and provided with a massive keep. This is in the inner of the two baileys or courtyards and here also were the hall and chambers which in the Middle Ages accommodated the king and the royal household on their visits to Carlisle. The keep still stands, but the hall and chambers have been swept away except for some masonry in the building now used as the museum of The Border Regiment and the King's Own Royal Border Regiment. At one end is a 14th-century staircase tower, named Queen Mary's Tower after Mary, Queen of Scots, who was imprisoned in the castle in 1568.

In the 16th century the upper part of the keep was rebuilt to provide a platform for cannon and its interior strengthened with new walls and vaults to support the heavier load. About the same time the walls of the inner bailey were greatly increased in width to take artillery, and a half-moon battery built outside its entrance. The design of the new defences was the work of Stephan von Haschenperg, a surveyor, originally from Moravia, who was employed by Henry VIII as a military engineer. As well as the work at the castle he also supervised new works on the city walls, not as extensive as those at Berwick (49,N), nor of the same type, but inspired by the same need for protection against artillery.

Within the keep are carvings by prisoners who during their captivity scraped designs on the walls of their cells, some skilfully wrought, others crudely scratched on the stonework. Also in the keep is a modern exhibition tracing the history of Border warfare.

On leaving the castle observe the two gatehouses. Both are defended by heavy doors and portcullises and originally had drawbridges on their outer sides, across

moats. The contract for building the outer gatehouse is dated 1378 and names John Lewyn, a master mason from Durham, as the builder and, in effect, designer. The barracks and storehouses around the parade ground were built in the 19th century when the castle was a regimental depot. Military occupation continued until 1959. Indeed there is still a small military presence.

The City Walls. Castle and city are now separated by a modern double carriageway, but in medieval times the city walls were continuous with those of the castle to form one secure defensive unit. Although there were periods of neglect, the walls were still sufficiently intact in the 17th century to withstand a prolonged siege during the Civil War, the Royalist garrison being compelled to surrender by starvation rather than by force of arms. In 1745 the city's defences were again put to the test when it was captured and held for a time by Charles Edward Stuart the 'Young Pretender'. On this occasion the walls succumbed to the heavy cannon of the duke of Cumberland. It was the last siege of any English city, ironically by an English army.

The surviving parts of the walls are

Market-place, Carlisle. JOHN BETHELL

best seen from the gardens and car park below West Walls. Here there is a continuous length which, despite the loss of battlements and some diminution in height, still gives a good impression of the size and scale of the defences.

There were three gates into the city, all now removed. To the west, near the castle, was Caldew or Irish Gate; towards the north-east, facing the bridge across the Eden, stood Ricker or Scotch Gate; and at the southern extremity was Botcher Gate or English Gate. In the 16th century Botcher Gate was replaced by a fortress designed by von Haschenperg which had a central square tower and flanking round towers designed to take artillery. A new gate was made to one side. The ghost of this fortress or citadel can be seen in the towers built on the same site in the 19th century as assize courts and prison and now housing county courts and offices. Indeed some 16th-century masonry still remains in the lower levels of the eastern tower.

The Cathedral is in the western half of the city. It began as the priory church of an Augustinian monastery founded by Henry I. In 1133 Henry made it the see of a bishop and until the Dissolution it was, like Durham, both cathedral and priory church, with the cloister and living quarters of the monks on its south side. It is a somewhat lop-sided building, all but two bays of its nave having been demolished in the 17th century by the city authorities, who at that time were responsible for the upkeep of the nave and eventually refused to pay for its repair.

What appears at first sight to be the nave is the choir of the medieval church, a handsome structure built from 1292 onwards and filled with light from its great east window. Of particular interest are the 15th-century choir stalls and screens which have their original misericords. Of even greater rarity is the Salkeld screen on the south side of the choir, given about 1541 by Lancelot Salkeld, last prior and first dean of the cathedral. Its carved decoration is not gothic but classical, and it is one of the few examples of early English Renaissance decoration, not just in the North but in the country as a whole, a precious survival. The two bays of the 12th-century nave are now used as the chapel of the Border Regiment.

In the cloister the whole of the refectory range still stands. The refectory itself was at first floor level above a vaulted basement which has been made, very successfully, into a restaurant and bookshop. Further to the west is the Deanery, once the prior's lodging, and beyond this is the priory gatehouse. It has the typical arrangement of separate entrances for wagons and pedestrians. A short walk away, with access either from West Walls or from the market-place, is the priory's tithe barn, once within the outer court. It was built in the 15th century and has been restored from a dilapidated state after use as a smithy.

The City. At the heart of the city is the market-place, possibly on the same site as the Roman forum. On its north side is the Town Hall, a modest, homely structure built in 1717 on the site of an earlier town hall. In front of it is the market-cross. Nearby is the Guildhall, the headquarters of the city's eight guilds: Merchants, Butchers, Shoemakers, Taylors, Smiths, Skinners, Weavers and Tanners. It is timber-framed, as indeed were most of the buildings of the city until the 17th century. More substantial houses began to appear towards the end of that century, such as Tullie House, built by Thomas Tullie in 1689 and now part of the city's museum and art gallery, and during the 18th century more of the city was rebuilt. There are, for example, agreeable Georgian houses in Abbey Street, Castle Street and Fisher Street, between cathedral and castle.

For the most part, all new building took place within the bounds of the city walls. A plan of the city in 1770 shows it very much as it was 200 years earlier, with the same street plan (still recognisable today) and with only very small suburbs planted outside the city gates. In the early part of the 19th century, however, the need to expand was overwhelming. On the north-east and east sides the city walls were pulled down and a new suburb formed with Lowther Street as its base. To the south-west, where some industrial activity had

already started, using the River Caldew for water power, a new industrial suburb rapidly developed, fostered by the opening of the canal to Port Carlisle and, later, by the coming of the railways. The first to arrive, in 1836, was the Newcastle and Carlisle Railway and by the 1870s seven companies were running services into the city. The canal has been filled in but Sir William Tite's handsome railway station of 1847–8 still serves the modern traveller. Among the city's industrial buildings, Dixon's Mill, now the Shaddon Works, is outstanding, built in 1836 as a cotton mill and a structure of monumental grandeur.

66
Durham, County Durham

OS 88 NZ 2742

In the year 995 the monks of Lindisfarne left their refuge at Chester-le-Street (D) in search of greater security. Carrying with them the coffin of St Cuthbert, they settled finally in the valley of the River Wear, on a strip of high ground protected on three sides by a loop of the river. Here they founded a monastery and built a church, the 'white church', which was dedicated on 4 September 998. This was the predecessor of the great cathedral that stands on the same site, the burial place of St Cuthbert and the most splendid Romanesque building in Europe.

The Cathedral. The 'white church' was used for nearly 100 years. It was removed in 1093 to make way for a new cathedral and a new monastery, and it is these one sees today.

By 1133 the cathedral was virtually complete. Nave, crossing, transepts and choir were all built in the first forty years and follow a single consistent design. The architecture is simple and uncomplicated. The effect is overwhelming. Inside the church the giant columns of the nave and choir, the soaring vaults, and the carving of the stonework give an unforgettable impression of uncompromising strength and authority.

The Galilee chapel was added to the west end in the later years of the 12th

century, and in the 13th century the east end was rebuilt on a larger scale to form the Chapel of the Nine Altars. The west window of the nave was inserted about 1360 and the great central tower was raised to its present height during the course of the 15th century. They add to the glories of the building, but it is the Norman architecture of the body of the cathedral that provides the dominant and most memorable image.

The coffin of St Cuthbert, removed from the 'white church' was kept in a temporary shrine in the north-west corner of the cloisters during the first years of rebuilding, but in 1104 it was placed behind the high altar in a shrine that became an object of pilgrimage and veneration. At the Dissolution the shrine was destroyed and the coffin buried under a plain marble slab. In the Galilee chapel is another memorial of the early church in Northumbria. The bones of the Venerable Bede, taken from Jarrow in 1022, had been placed in the coffin of St Cuthbert. In 1370 they were removed to the Galilee and there reburied. The site is marked by a stone tomb covered with black marble.

After the Dissolution many of the cathedral's fittings and nearly all its woodwork were destroyed, much of it in 1650 when 4,000 Scottish prisoners were confined in the cathedral. The magnificent Nevill screen behind the high altar and the tomb of Bishop Hatfield under the bishop's throne are among the few items surviving from the years of destruction; also the early 16th-century clock in the south transept, remodelled in 1630 and restored to its original position in 1938. The choir stalls and screen were provided by Bishop Cosin in the 17th century to replace some of the missing woodwork. A further example of his sumptuous woodwork is the canopy over the font in the nave.

The Cloisters and College Green. The cloisters of the Benedictine monastery and the living quarters of the monks lay on the south side of the cathedral and many of the buildings still survive, now put to different uses. On the east side of the cloister is the chapter house; on the south side are the refectory and kitchen, now the cathedral library and muniment

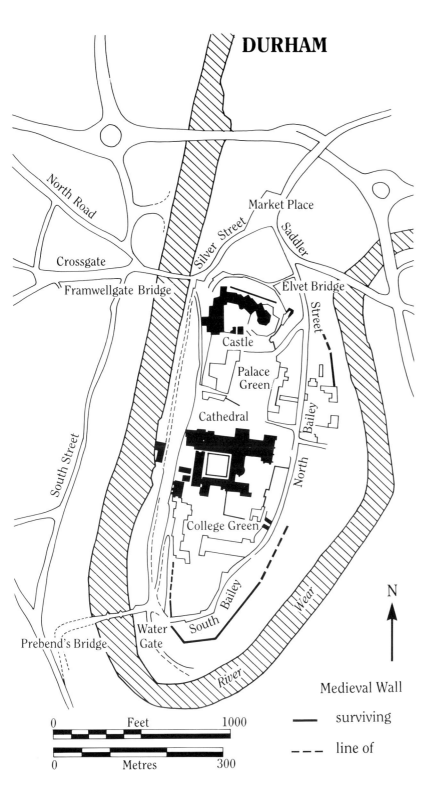

DURHAM

North Road

Market Place

Crossgate

Silver Street

Saddler

Framwellgate Bridge

Elvet Bridge

Street

Castle

Palace
Green

North Bailey

Cathedral

South Street

College Green

South Bailey

Wear

River

Prebend's Bridge

Water
Gate

N

Medieval Wall

```
0        Feet        1000
0        Metres      300
```

—— surviving

- - - line of

Durham (after RAI). EH

room; and on the west side is the monks' dormitory, built in the early part of the 15th century to replace an earlier dormitory in the east range. A collection of early stone sculptures and grave slabs is on display in the dormitory, and an exhibition of the cathedral's treasures is in one of the vaulted chambers below. They include the remarkable 12th-century door knocker once on the north door of the cathedral and now replaced by a replica to avoid further deterioration. (See also entry 24.)

Beyond the cloister is College Green or 'The College', once the outer court of the monastery and now rebuilt with houses for the cathedral clergy and the choir school. It also has a pretty little octagonal tower, built in 1751 as a water reservoir.

The Castle stands to the north of the cathedral where the peninsula is at its narrowest. It was built in 1072 by Waltheof, earl of Northumberland, but it was not the first fortification. Earlier defences, sufficiently strong to withstand sieges by the Scots in 1006 and 1038, were already in position, protecting the Lindisfarne community and the early monastery, but nothing of these survives.

The Norman castle was given by William the Conqueror to Bishop Walcher, and for more than 700 years it was the principal fortress and residence of the bishops of Durham, who in the Middle Ages exercised both civil and ecclesiastical power in their domain, holding their own parliaments, issuing their own coinage, and licensing castles, as well as maintaining their high office in the Church. It began as a motte and bailey castle with a high mound, which still survives, and with an accompanying courtyard in which stood the principal buildings. During the course of the Middle Ages these were gradually rebuilt to provide greater comfort, but a remarkable amount of the early castle still remains including an 11th-century chapel.

On the west side of the courtyard, is the great hall built by Bishop Bek about 1300 and south-west of this is the castle kitchen which is still in use. North of the hall is the Black Staircase built by Bishop Cosin in 1662 which led to private chambers in the north range. In part of the north range is a magnificent 12th-century doorway and, at a higher level, the remains of the Constable's Hall. There are two chapels, one made by the Bishop Tunstall in the 1540s, the other built in the 11th century. It is small and primitive but marvellously expressive of the earliest period of Norman occupation.

In 1836 the castle was given to the newly founded University of Durham and became a residential college. Few changes were made to the domestic quarters but the medieval shell-keep on top of the mound, which had fallen into ruin, was rebuilt about 1840 to the design of Anthony Salvin and made into student accommodation. Many of the

buildings around Palace Green also passed to the University. They occupy what was once the outer bailey of the castle, defended by a gatehouse at the head of Saddler Street. Indeed the whole of the upper part of the hill, including the cathedral and monastic buildings, was formerly surrounded by a fortified wall, which together with the other defences made this promontory in medieval times a huge and powerful citadel.

The Market-Place and beyond. North of the castle and below its walls was the medieval market-place and associated streets. The area was itself walled in the early 14th century, as a protection against the Scots. Many of the present buildings have 18th and 19th-century frontages but among them are a few timber-framed structures earlier in date.

Medieval bridges span the river to the

east and to the west. To the east is Elvet bridge, built in the 12th century and formerly with two chapels. It was doubled in width in 1805. Framwellgate bridge, to the west, dates from about 1400 and was widened in 1856.

Beyond the bridges there are some attractive 18th-century houses and, for an excellent view of the castle and cathedral, a walk along South Street on the west bank of the river is recommended. From South Street one can descend to the 18th-century Prebend's Bridge and then have the choice of following the river bank to the Old Fulling Mill, which houses the university's archaeological collections, or of ascending through the Watergate and along the South Bailey, enjoying the variety of buildings in this pleasant street. In St Mary le Bow, North Bailey, is an exhibition devoted to local history.

Durham cathedral from the north. AFK

Plate 1 *Castlerigg Stone Circle.*
NT/MIKE WILLIAMS

Plate 2 *Hadrian's Wall. Aerial view of Housesteads fort.*
AEROFILMS

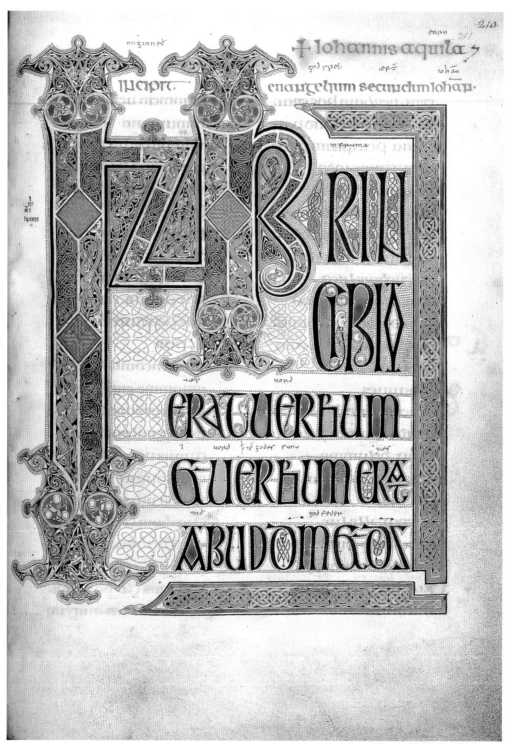

Plate 3 *Lindisfarne Gospels. The opening page of St John's Gospel.* BRITISH LIBRARY

Plate 4 *Durham from the air.*
AEROFILMS

Plate 5 *Berwick-upon-Tweed from the air.* AEROFILMS

Plate 6 *Durham cathedral. The nave.* JOHN BETHELL

Plate 7 *Gibside chapel.* A F KERSTING

Plate 8 *Lakeland farmhouse and spinning gallery. Yew Tree farm, Cumbria.* NT

Plate 9 *Levens Hall. The topiary garden in spring.*
JOHN BETHELL

Plate 10 The Opening of the Stockton and Darlington Railway, *1825, by John Dobbin.* BOROUGH OF DARLINGTON MUSEUM

Plate 11 *Beam-engines at Ryhope pumping station.* RYHOPE ENGINES TRUST

Plate 12 *Wallington Hall. The saloon.* NT/HORST KOLO

67

Hexham, Northumberland
Middle Ages and later

OS 87 NY 935642. 20 miles (32km)
W of Newcastle on A69

Hexham began as a cluster of huts at the gate of a 7th-century monastery. It was sacked by the Danes and laid waste by William the Conqueror, but in the 12th and 13th centuries it developed into a market-town under the walls of its medieval priory. Its lay-out is haphazard. At the heart of the town is the market-place with a network of roads leading into it, all medieval in origin except Beaumont Street, which was made in the 19th century. A second focus of development is further south along the Newcastle to Carlisle road, named Priestpopple and Battle Hill as it passes through the town.

West of the market-place was the Augustinian priory founded in 1113 on the site of the early monastery (see 27). During the Middle Ages it was separated from the market-place by its precinct wall and other buildings, but these were removed in the 19th century bringing the east end of the church prominently into view.

The town was not fortified but on the east side of the market-place was the stronghold of the archbishops of York, owners until 1572 of the regality of Hexhamshire, that is to say of most of the surrounding lands. The most prominent building is the Moot Hall, built in the 15th century as a fortified gatehouse, and beyond, in what was formerly a walled enclosure, is a second powerful tower, dating from 1330–2. Gatehouse and tower housed the archbishop's officers, his exchequer, his court, and his prison.

Frequently attacked and burned by the Scots from 1296 onwards, little else of the medieval town survives. There are fragments of the parish church of St Mary's in St Mary's Chare, but the majority of the town's buildings are from the 17th century and later. Its increasing prosperity is reflected in the houses of Market Street, Gilesgate, Fore Street and Battle Hill, and in the

Hexham. AFK

Grammar School built in 1684. The bridge across the Tyne, half a mile (0.8km) to the north, a handsome structure disfigured by modern widening, was designed by Robert Mylne and completed in 1788.

Primarily an agricultural centre for the surrounding district, Hexham had a flourishing tanning industry and leather trade, and in the 19th century was noted for its glove-making. There was also some woollen manufacture and hat making. Its four guilds were those of the Weavers, Hatters, Tanners and Shoemakers, and Skinners and Glovers. The Shambles, a covered market on the south of the market-place, was built in 1766 at the expense of Sir Walter Calverley Blackett, lord of the manor.

At the Dissolution the priory was closed but the church was spared to become the parish church in place of St Mary's. The crossing, transepts, and chancel, except for its east end, survive from the medieval church built between 1180 and 1250. Of exceptional interest is the night stair in the south transept which permitted the monks to enter the church direct from their dormitory for the night services. Of great rarity also is the timber screen separating the chancel

from the crossing. It was installed during the rule of Prior Smithson between 1491 and 1524. The crypt and other early remains are described in entry 27.

The nave was built in 1907–9 and designed by Temple Moore. The cloister of the priory and the living quarters of the monks were on the south side of the church but only a few fragments survive. However, to the north of the church is the priory gate, 12th-century in date and formerly two-storeyed. It was the principal entrance to the priory whose grounds extended from here to the church and included the land to the south-west, now a public park.

68

Kendal, Cumbria
Middle Ages and later

OS 97 SD 514925. On A6 between Lancaster and Penrith. Junctions 36 or 37 on M6

Writing at the end of the 17th century the Revd Thomas Machell described Kendal as 'a most famous town for its industry and the woollen trade', and from the later Middle Ages onwards, until eclipsed by the output of mills further south, the making of woollen cloth and the knitting of stockings were two of the principal occupations of the inhabitants of Kendal and its immediate hinterland. Its 'Kendal green' cloth was known throughout England. It prospered also as a market, serving an area that extended from Furness in the west to Kirkby Stephen in the upper valley of the Eden. As a transport centre, it supplied the smaller towns and villages by packhorse and wagon and provided a regular service to Carlisle, Newcastle and London.

At the Conquest, 'Kentdale' was granted to Ivo de Taillebois, and the motte and bailey castle in the south-west quarter of the town is evidence of Norman occupation. In 1086 there is mention of a church, and in the 11th and 12th centuries the principal area of settlement was probably between the early castle and the present church of Holy Trinity in the southern part of the town. Subsequently the focus moved further north and a market-place was established at the junction of the principal roads, with houses and burgage plots on both sides of the main thoroughfares, Highgate, Stricklandgate and Stramongate. The river lay to the east, probably with fords on or near the sites of the present bridges.

Until the 17th century many of the burgage plots remained open and semi-rural behind the street frontages, but already some had been partly filled with workshops and lodgings for artisans. During the 18th and 19th centuries the former open spaces became narrow yards flanked by buildings and entered by archways from the street. This distinctive network survived until recent times, but much has been obliterated by modern development and in many instances all that remains as a reminder of the earlier pattern is an entrance arch under the roadside building.

The town was not walled. It relied for its protection on a later castle established on the hill east of the river and held in the later Middle Ages by Sir William de Parr and his descendants, one of whom was Catherine Parr, sixth and last wife of Henry VIII. This castle,

Highgate, Kendal. CL

replacing the earlier motte and bailey on the west side of the valley, was founded probably at the end of the 12th century but, although its defences can still be traced, little of its internal masonry survives. The town also benefitted from its distance from the Scottish border. Evidence of its comparative security is provided by a 14th-century house, now known as Castle Dairy, on the outskirts of the town near Stramongate bridge, which has a central hall and cross wings and which, unlike other northern manor houses, shows no sign of fortification.

Most of the domestic buildings of the town are 18th-century or later, and built of stone. Few of the landed gentry of the county built houses in the town and only Abbot Hall, built in 1759 by the Wilsons of Dallam Tower to the design of John Carr of York, and now an excellent art gallery and museum, is a notable work of architecture. The town was dominated by trade, and its buildings exhibit a sober and undemonstrative character with few embellishments. Sandes Hospital in Highgate was founded by Thomas Sandes in 1670 for eight poor widows and although much of it was rebuilt in 1852 the gatehouse range is part of the original structure.

A minor industry was the making of snuff using at first the powder and broken stalks from tobacco imported at Whitehaven and brought by packhorse

through the Lake District to Penrith and Kendal. A snuff mill is recorded in the town in 1740 and the manufacture is still maintained. The earlier workshops and warehouses were in the eastern part between Highgate and Stramongate and the river. However, in the early part of the 19th century land across the river, hitherto mainly agricultural, began to be developed, stimulated by the opening of the Lancaster to Kendal canal in 1818. Wharves and warehouses were built around the canal basin, and some still survive although the canal itself has been filled in.

A branch line of the Lancaster to Carlisle railway was laid from Oxenholme in 1846, bringing better communications to the town and, extending to Windermere, conveying tourists in ever increasing numbers to the Lake District. The present station was built in 1861.

69

Keswick, Cumbria
16th century and later

OS 90 NY 265235. 18 miles (29km) W of Penrith on A66. Junction 40 on M6

In 1564 the Company of Mines Royal was founded by Queen Elizabeth I to increase and extend the mining of 'gold, silver, copper and quicksilver' in England and Wales, and to bring German miners to this country in order to benefit from their skills and experience. Within a few years a colony of German miners was established in and near Keswick, and mines worked by them were operating in Borrowdale and in Newlands Valley to the west, where the most profitable copper mine was named *Gotes Gab* (God's gift) or, in the English vernacular, Goldscope. A smelter and refinery were built at Brigham near the River Greta, three quarters of a mile (1.2km) north-east of Keswick.

The Company collapsed in 1579, but the mining of copper and lead continued in the area until the later part of the 19th century, as did the mining of graphite, first discovered at Seathwaite in 1555. It was used in industry and medicine and, from the 18th century, for the manufacture of pencils. The Cumberland Pencil Company is still in the town and has a museum near its present works at Greta Bridge.

John Leland, in the early years of the 16th century, described Keswick as a 'poor lytle market town'. Mining brought prosperity and a wider range of trades, and in 1571 the town built a Moot Hall in the centre of the main street, since rebuilt in the 19th century. Several of the buildings in the centre of the town have facades of the 18th and early 19th century, but behind the frontages are older parts and the pattern of yards and alleys is a survival from the earlier town.

With the 19th century came tourism and expansion. The Cockermouth, Keswick and Penrith Railway was opened in 1865 and the Keswick Hotel, near the former station, dates from 1869. Both town and countryside reflect the growing popularity of Borrowdale for a more leisured population. Sedate

Edwardian boarding houses were built in the town, hotels in the valleys, and, for those retiring to live in the district, a swarm of Italianate villas spread among the foothills.

Greta Hall, now a boarding house for Keswick School, was the home of two of the town's most famous residents, Samuel Taylor Coleridge, for a short time, and Robert Southey, for more than forty years. William and Dorothy Wordsworth were among the visitors to the house, as were Shelley, De Quincey, Hazlitt and Charles and Mary Lamb. Southey is buried in the graveyard of Crosthwaite church, a mile (0.6km) from the centre of the town and dedicated to St Kentigern, known in Scotland as St Mungo. Here also is buried Canon Rawnsley, vicar of Crosthwaite from 1888 to 1917. Co-founder in 1895 of the National Trust, he was a passionate conserver of the Lake District and its traditions. The Keswick museum and art gallery is in Fitz Park, on the north-eastern side of the town.

70

Lowther, Cumbria
17th and 18th centuries

OS 90 NY 528242 and 538236.
Penrith. 5 miles (8km) S of Penrith on A6 and minor roads

Lowther castle is a huge, gothic mansion designed by George Dance and Robert Smirke for the 1st earl of Lonsdale and built between 1802 and 1814. It is now empty and roofless although its walls still stand, making it a spectacular ruin in the surrounding park. It is the last of a series of houses on the site which began with a medieval tower house. Medieval also is St Michael's church nearby, though its exterior is the work of Sir John Lowther in 1686.

Sir John pulled down the old village of Lowther and built the grandly named Lowther Newtown just east of castle and church. It consists of a small group of terraced houses, two-storeyed and plainly treated, with the 'College' at the north end. This was built as a manufactory for the employment of the poor. Later it became a school, then a manufactory again, and finally the estate office.

Altogether more ambitious is a second estate village about half a mile (0.75km) to the south-east. It was designed on classical lines by the architect Robert Adam for Sir James Lowther, later the 1st earl of Lonsdale, and started about 1765. The houses are grouped symmetrically in terraces, with two groups in open-ended squares and the third group forming a crescent of single-storey houses with taller pavilions at the ends. The original designs, preserved in the Soane Museum, London, show a much larger lay-out, and, apparently, a second crescent was built, making a complete ring, but this was later demolished.

Richard Warner in his *Tour through the Northern Counties*, published in 1802, commented on the 'fantastical' incongruity of its plan, which exhibits the grandest features of city architecture, the Circus, the Crescent, and the Square, upon the mean scale of

Keswick and Skiddaw. J ALLAN CASH

Lowther village. EDWIN SMITH

a peasant's cottage.' An uncharitable view of housing that is neat and agreeable, and greatly superior to most rural cottages of the time.

71

Newcastle upon Tyne, Tyne and Wear

OS 88 NZ 2464

[A] EH (Bessie Surtees House)

The southern approach to Newcastle is memorable. Suddenly one crosses the Tyne at a great height with the river flowing between steep-sided banks. Immediately in front are the buildings of the city spreading out as far as the eye can see along the river bank and on the high ground to the north. It is an unexpected and breath-taking sight. Equally dramatic is the approach at a lower level, crossing the river on the Swing Bridge with the higher bridges soaring overhead.

The Swing Bridge is on the site of a Roman bridge, Pons Aelius, named in honour of the emperor Hadrian, whose family name was Aelius. Above it, on the north bank, on a bluff above the river,

was a Roman fort built to guard the river crossing. It was also, at first, the eastern terminus of Hadrian's Wall, becoming part of the general defences when the wall was soon extended eastwards to Wallsend.

The 'New Castle on the Tyne', from which the city takes its name, occupies the same site as the Roman fort. It was founded in 1080 by Robert, eldest son of William the Conqueror, and it became one of the most powerful in the north, controlling the Tyne valley and barring the way south against the Scots. Under its protection a large and thriving town developed with its own circuit of walls and towers.

The ending of Border hostilities improved its trade and commerce, and with the increasing export of coal from the Tyne the town grew in wealth and importance. Piecemeal development brought Georgian squares and terraces, but, in the first half of the 19th century, bold and imaginative planning created a new town centre of great elegance, with wide streets lined with classical frontages and municipal buildings of considerable grandeur.

During the 19th century Newcastle and its satellite towns developed into one of the greatest concentrations of heavy industry in the world, and to

many people, perhaps, the picture of Tyneside is one of shipyards, blast-furnaces, engineering shops, and chemical works. To them a walk round Newcastle will be a revelation. There are still substantial remains of the medieval town, occasional glimpses of Tudor and 17th-century Newcastle, and much Georgian elegance. The commercial centre is still regulated by the spacious planning of the 19th century, and in Grey Street the city possesses one of the most majestic streets in Britain. It is a city of great variety and extraordinary interest.

The Castle is now in two parts divided by the main London to Edinburgh railway. South of the viaduct is the 12th-century keep built on the orders of Henry II and designed by 'Maurice the Engineer', who a few years later built the great keep at Dover castle in Kent for the same king. It is slightly smaller than the Dover keep but equally ingenious in its planning.

The principal chamber is at the second floor level reached by an external staircase, which is defended by three towers. The present fireplace is 16th-century and the vault was inserted in the 19th century, but the chamber was always of great height with an upper gallery contained within the thicknesses of the walls. Leading from the large chamber are smaller rooms, the 'King's Chamber' on the south and, in the north-east corner, a room which has a well and was used perhaps as a kitchen. In the west wall are passages to latrines.

At first floor level is a second central chamber with a smaller room, the 'Queen's Chamber' on the north side. At ground level are a chapel and a large vaulted hall which in later times was used as a prison.

The massiveness of the building and the carefully controlled access made it particularly secure. Its careful planning also provided two sets of self-contained chambers, appropriately guarded and well appointed. They may have been for royal use when the king and his household stayed at the castle. The history of the castle is displayed in an exhibition in the keep and for a panoramic view of the city it is worth ascending to the roof.

Near the keep and outlined on the ground are the sites of buildings belonging to the Roman fort. Here too were found the graves of a Christian cemetery of about AD 700. North of the viaduct is the Black Gate, built in 1247 to improve the defences of the castle entrance. It had drawbridges both to the front and rear. In 1618 its upper part, then ruinous, was rebuilt to provide a house whose brick walls and mullion and transom windows rise above the medieval stonework. It now houses an antiquarian library and a bag-pipe museum. Nearby is the Heron Pit, once a prison.

The Cathedral and other Churches. North of the castle is St Nicholas's cathedral, made the seat of a bishop in 1882 and previously one of the city's parish churches. Parts date from the 12th and 13th centuries but most of the building is late medieval with a considerable amount of 19th-century restoration. Its most remarkable feature

is its west tower which has a 'crown' of flying buttresses supporting an open lantern. Its striking silhouette is a landmark in the city despite the modern buildings round about.

Other medieval churches in the city are St Andrew's and St John's, and of later date is the handsome church of All Saints, built in 1786–96 to the design of David Stephenson. It has an oval nave and a galleried interior but is no longer in ecclesiastical use. Near the station is the 19th-century Roman Catholic cathedral designed by A W N Pugin but with a later spire.

Although little of the medieval church of the Dominican friary survives, other parts of the friary still remain. The Dominicans or Black Friars were established in Newcastle before 1239. When closed in 1539 the buildings were purchased by the Mayor and burgesses and leased to the town guilds who converted the domestic ranges into meeting halls and living quarters. The

site of the church has been excavated and its remains displayed, and an imaginative scheme of repair and renovation by the City Council has preserved the cloister and medieval ranges. They are now used as craft shops, exhibition areas and a restaurant. One of the guild halls is also on display. It is west of the city centre, near the medieval town wall.

The Town Walls. More survives of the medieval walls of Newcastle than of any other English town, save York, Chester and Southampton. They enclose an area of 150 acres, (60.7ha), are two miles (5.18km) in circumference and, originally, had seven principal gates and a number of posterns. There were nineteen towers, of which eight survive, and between the towers, small turrets or watch towers, sufficiently large to accommodate a single bowman.

The walls were severely damaged during the Civil War, holding out for Charles I against a Scottish army under

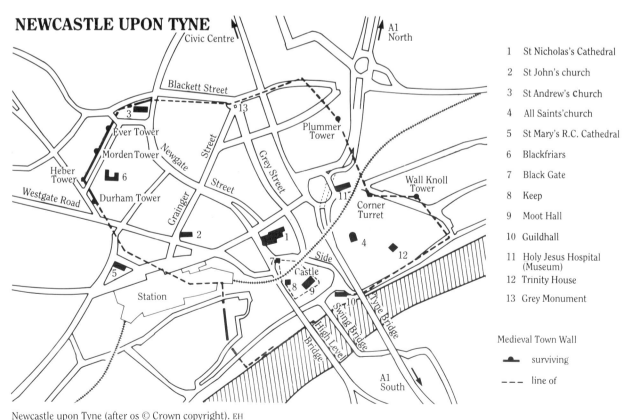

Newcastle upon Tyne (after os © Crown copyright). EH

1   St Nicholas's Cathedral

2   St John's church

3   St Andrew's church

4   All Saints'church

5   St Mary's R.C. Cathedral

6   Blackfriars

7   Black Gate

8   Keep

9   Moot Hall

10   Guildhall

11   Holy Jesus Hospital (Museum)

12   Trinity House

13   Grey Monument

General Leslie, and parts were demolished in the 19th century, including all the gates. However, several lengths still stand to an impressive height especially on the west and north-west sides, and a walk along their route with a plan or guide is a very rewarding exercise, both for historians and for those interested in the quieter corners of urban life. The walls were begun before 1264 and, with an extension on the eastern side, completed by about 1300.

Town and City. A tour of historic Newcastle could begin on the riverside near the Swing Bridge which is also the site of the Roman and medieval bridges across the Tyne. From here there is a good view of Stephenson's High Level

Bridge (103). Nearby, in Sandhill, is the Guildhall. Its present facades are classical, added in the late 18th and early 19th centuries, but the rooms inside are 17th-century, the work of Robert Trollope. Its medieval predecessor was a fortified tower house. Also in Sandhill are several timber-framed buildings, including the romantically named 'Bessie Surtees House', five-storeyed and many windowed and now in the care of English Heritage. Similar houses are shown on early views of Newcastle clustered along the river and especially on Quayside. This was the trading and commercial heart of the town, a medley of merchants' houses and warehouses with narrow 'chares' or alleyways,

leading back from the quay to the steep bank behind. Flights of steps then ascended the bank to the upper parts of the town.

Victorian shipping offices survive along Quayside, and other memorials of a vigorous maritime trade are the 18th-century Custom House and, round the corner in Broad Chare, Trinity House, whose sober 19th-century frontage hides an 18th-century quadrangle with hall, chapel, school and almshouses. Nearby is the Trinity Maritime Centre with exhibitions of maritime history.

Returning to Sandhill, the principal route from the medieval bridge to the higher parts of the town was The Side, making its ascent under the walls of the castle and past St Nicholas's Cathedral to the street markets immediately north: Cloth Market, Groat Market, and Bigg (formerly Oat) Market. Further on, Bigg Market became Newgate Street heading north to one of the medieval gates, now destroyed. West of Newgate Street are Blackfriars and some of the best preserved lengths of town wall, beginning in St Andrew's churchyard.

To the east are the streets of the new town, built between 1835 and 1839. This great enterprise was mainly the work of three men, the builder and entrepreneur Richard Grainger, the architect John Dobson, and John Clayton, Town Clerk. The most complete and best preserved of the new streets is Grey Street, but side streets and others nearby, such as Grainger Street and Pilgrim Street, are all part of the grand design. In the last thirty years parts have been destroyed by eccentric planning and unsuitable new buildings, but the general character and lay-out still survive. It is described by Pevsner in his guide to Northumberland as 'the best designed Victorian town in England'.

The covered markets in Grainger Street are worth a visit and Dobson's railway station, a little away from the centre because of the lie of the land, is not to be missed. Another building of great character and interest is the 17th-century Holy Jesus Hospital, built as an almshouse and now the John George Joicey Museum. It is one of several excellent museums and art galleries in the city.

Tyne bridges, Newcastle upon Tyne. AEROFILMS

72

Ogle, Northumberland
Middle Ages and later

OS 88 NZ 137791. 14 miles
(22.5km) NW of Newcastle
on A696 and minor road
[D]

In 1341 Robert de Ogle was granted a
licence to fortify his manor house at
Ogle, and in 1415 it is described as the
'castrum de Ogill'. Part of its moat still
survives and some of the present house
may be medieval, but most of it is later.
It stands on its own, north-east of a
small cluster of houses and farms, and
separated from them by a large field.
This field, however, was once the village
green of a much larger community
shown on a plan of 1632 with rows of
houses on the north and south sides of
the green, each house standing on its
own croft. Beyond these were the village
fields.

What is drawn on the plan is
confirmed by aerial photography. The
outline of the medieval village stands
out clearly against the ridge and furrow
of the surrounding fields, and the
positions of the houses and their crofts
are registered as earthworks on both
sides of the long central space. The
manor house is in the trees to the left.

By 1830 the once extensive village

Ogle village from the north. CUCAP

had shrunk to a group of farms and
cottages in the south-west corner of the
green, with some new farmsteads
further out and with a new road cutting
through the southern part of the green.
The reasons for the decline are not
recorded, but the new pattern of
settlement points to an improving
landowner who divided the village land
into separate farmsteads for the better
exploitation of his estate. It deprived the

villagers of their means of subsistence
and forced them off the land.

In the 19th and early 20th centuries
there was further shrinkage, reversed
only in recent times by the building of
new houses to the north of the road.
They encroach on part of the former
green but the greater part of the
medieval village is still deserted and
untouched, a silent record of an earlier
pattern of life.

7

Country Life

For 300 years from about 1300 to 1600, the Border counties were exposed to pillage and destruction. Those who could afford to do so fortified their houses, and at **Aydon Castle** (73,N) one can see demonstrated in stone the transformation from defenceless manor house to fortified dwelling capable of withstanding local raids. Other landowners preferred to start afresh, building towers as their homes. Sometimes called 'peles' or 'pele towers', they are familiar sights throughout the area, but especially within twenty miles of the Scottish border, occasionally in clusters, elsewhere in isolation. Many are in ruins, others have been adapted and enlarged to provide more comfortable accommodation, becoming parts of stately homes whose Georgian facades discreetly hide their medieval ancestry (88,C).

Priests as well as secular lords were forced to seek protection. The Vicar's Pele at **Corbridge** (77,N) is the tower house of the parish priest with all his accommodation contained within its walls; others are at Elsdon (53,N), Embleton (N) and Alnham (N), although only at Corbridge is the interior readily accessible. Churches, also, were given powerful towers to serve as refuges, such as the one at **Newton Arlosh** (80,C), and the walls and gateways of monasteries were strengthened and fortified to protect their communities as, for example, at Lindisfarne (38,N).

On the eastern side of the Pennines the free-standing tower, compact and self-contained, is the dominant form. On the west, fortified towers are found attached to other ranges, with chambers in the tower but hall and kitchen in undefended parts. An excellent example is **Yanwath Hall** (84,C) and a similar arrangement existed at Sizergh (95,C) and at Levens (91,C). A few had two towers, flanking the central range. These substantial houses belonged to the wealthier members of society, but the same pressing need for defence is also found in the 'bastle houses' of the

area, dating from the 16th and early 17th centuries, where, as at **Black Middens** (75,N), the farmer and his family lived on the upper floor and his valuable animals were herded into the chamber below.

War and lawlessness persisted through the Tudor period, crippling the northern counties and putting them 100 years behind the southern parts of England. Whereas the 'great rebuilding' of houses began in the South in the 1570s, in the North it started on a large scale only in the 1670s. But once begun, it transformed the countryside, as may be seen from the spacious and solidly built houses of Cumbria, many bearing datestones of the late 17th and early 18th centuries on their doorways. **Townend** (81,C) at Troutbeck in Cumbria is a fine example of a 17th-century yeoman's dwelling, enlarged and improved as the fortunes of its owners increased. It has the great advantage of being open to visitors, being in the care of the National Trust.

Enclosure and agricultural improvement in the 18th and 19th centuries brought a further surge in building, and farmhouses of this period, late-Georgian in style, are prominent in the farming areas of Northumberland, often with farm buildings and farm cottages making small agricultural hamlets separate from the older villages. Enclosure, too, brought the stone walls of valley and moorland, forming a pattern of masonry which is one of the most memorable features of the northern uplands.

The coming of the railway transformed country life. Hitherto, cattle were moved across the countryside on a network of drove roads whose remains can still be followed in the hills (76,N), while packhorses were the mainstay of merchants and traders, their memorials being the simple stone bridges across the more turbulent streams (82,C).

The railways in turn have formed their own monuments, adding yet

Aydon castle. EH

another layer to the historical strata of the region. Some activities leave prominent remains; others are barely discernible. One whose imprint has almost disappeared is transhumance, the annual movement of stock to summer pastures, once widely practised in the northern hills. Its remains are remote and fragmentary, but few structures are more evocative of a vanished way of life (79,C).

73

Aydon Castle, Northumberland
Middle Ages and later

OS 87 NZ 002663. Corbridge.
1½ miles (2.4km) NE of Corbridge by B6321 and minor road

[A] EH

Aydon is hidden in woods above a small but steep ravine, a secretive and very beautiful place. It is a fortified house rather than a castle and at first had little to defend it other than its naturally strong position. It began as a hall-house of late-13th-century date with the hall at first floor level in the principal range and chambers in a cross-range at the east end. Later, the entrance was enclosed in a small courtyard behind battlemented walls and a new range added on the west. Finally, the walls of the outer courtyard were built, also a range of lodgings for guests and retainers in the south-west corner.

On other sites the answer to increasing lawlessness and attacks from the Scots was to build a strong tower for the owner and his household, the 'pele towers' that are scattered across the northern counties. At Aydon the existing house was fortified and enveloped in enclosing walls to give it an appropriate measure of protection.

Aydon was held by Robert de Reymes from 1296 to 1324 and later by his son, Robert. During this time the area was repeatedly attacked by the Scots and in 1313 Aydon was pillaged and burned. It was taken again in 1315, this time by local rebels, and by the Scots again in 1346. The later history of Aydon is a

Beadnell lime kilns. NT/MIKE WILLIAMS

series of attempts to adapt it to changing needs.

During Carnaby ownership in the 15th century partitions were inserted under the hall, and at the west end of the hall, to form additional rooms. In the 17th century the chamber block became the principal living area with the western parts of the house given up to farm use. Subsequently the house and farm buildings were let to tenant farmers and this remained its use until 1966. There was not at any time any major campaign of addition or rebuilding and this has been its salvation.

The farmhouse fittings have been stripped out leaving parts of the interior rather bare and cheerless, but its plan and architectural details are intact and as an example of medieval domestic architecture, armoured to meet the needs of the time, Aydon is unsurpassed.

74

Beadnell Lime Kilns, Northumberland
18th century

OS 75 NU 238285. Beadnell.
On coast 5 miles (8km) SE of Bamburgh. On quayside

[A] NT

Lime was used as a dressing for sour land in the 16th century, and by simple means, burning broken limestone in a turf-covered heap, small farmers provided their own supplies. Permanent stone-built kilns were introduced in the 18th century using local supplies of limestone and coal, and often built into hillsides to ease the task of top-loading. Their remains are scattered throughout the limestone uplands, in many cases reduced to little more than shapeless mounds but instantly recognisable by the tell-tale arch at the base of the surviving masonry.

In the second half of the 18th century larger kilns were built to serve a wider market. At Beadnell four kilns were in operation in the 1750s producing lime for local farms and also for export, but the present kilns on the quayside are later. The first was built by Richard Pringle under an agreement with the landowner, Thomas Wood, dated 23 November 1798. Wood had begun a new quay in the harbour the previous year, with a view to improving the local fishing industry, but also to help the export of coal, stone, lime and salt produced locally, and mainly on his land. His agreement with Pringle included an undertaking that the quay would be completed and kept in good repair during the term of the lease, and that Pringle for his part would pay Wood ninepence for each load of lime exported and sixpence for each load sold locally. Pringle also undertood to ship out 1,000 loads each years. Clearly the business prospered. New kilns were added to the original single kiln and they continued in operation until 1841.

Without a natural slope to help with loading, a ramp was built to take the

coal and limestone to the tops of the kilns, and tunnels made within the body of the kilns to give access to the hearths at the base from which the burnt lime was drawn. Parts of the structure on the seaward side have collapsed, but the rest has been repaired and is now in the care of the National Trust.

A fine battery of kilns is at Seahouses, 2 miles (3.2km) further north along the coast, and there are others on Holy Island (38,N).

75

Black Middens Bastle House, Northumberland
16th–early 17th century

OS 80 NY 774900. Tarset. 6 miles (9.6km) NW of Bellingham on minor road beyond Gatehouse

[A] EH

'Bastles' or 'bastle houses' are fortified farmhouses of a type only to be found in the northern counties and generally within 20 miles (32km) of the Scottish border. They are invariably two-storeyed and their distinctive characteristic is that they provided shelter for farm

animals on the ground floor and for their owners on the floor above.

Black Middens is a typical example and more accessible than most, being in the care of English Heritage, but those passing through the hamlet of Gatehouse will see two others close together on opposite sides of the road. Entrance to the living quarters is at first floor level by means of an external stone staircase, probably replacing an earlier ladder, leading to a doorway which was secured internally by a wooden draw-bar. The tunnel for the bar is to be seen in the thickness of the wall. The windows are few and deliberately small and often guarded by iron bars. There were two rooms at Black Middens, the larger of which had a fireplace, probably with a smoke hood made of timber and plaster, and in some instances, though not apparently here, there was a loft over the smaller room.

At ground floor level the two doorways flanking the staircase are modern. The original entrance is in the east wall. Some bastles had a stone barrel vault at ground floor level. Others, like Black Middens, had timber beams probably carrying stone flags, and with a hole for a ladder to provide access from one floor to another.

Unlike pele towers there is no provision for active defence. There are no wall-walks, battlements, or arrow slits. Bastles gave a passive form of protection against marauding bands, their occupants sheltering behind thick walls and barred doors until help came from friends and neighbours. Without an internal well, they relied on relief being speedy. Bastles date from the late 16th to the early 17th century, a period of general lawlessness along the border when those with property had to fend for themselves and provide their own protection.

Many are now ruinous and at Black Middens the roofs and floors are missing. It is, nevertheless, a good example of its type and has an appropriate position in a wild and remote part of the hills. There are walls nearby of unknown date but probably belonging to later farm buildings and 70 yards (64 m) to the north-east are the remains of another bastle.

Black Middens bastle house. EH

76

Clennell Street Drove Road, Northumberland
Middle Ages and later

OS 80 NT 852185 (Cocklawfoot) to NT 922064 (Alwinton). Alwinton is 9 miles (14.5km) NW of Rothbury by B6341 and minor roads

[A]

Clennell Street is one of the many drove roads from Scotland to England across the Cheviots. Its greatest use for droving was in the 18th and early 19th centuries but its origins are much older. It may have been a trading route in prehistoric and Roman times, and certainly by the early 12th century it was a well established cross-country track, referred to as 'the great road to Yarnspeth'. It was also used for transhumance. In the 12th century the flocks of Newminster Abbey were being driven along parts of it to summer pastures at Kidland, on land now covered by modern forest. During the centuries of Border warfare it was used by cattle reivers (rustlers), and in later times it provided an unobtrusive route across the hills for whisky smugglers slipping their wares into England.

The track crosses the border near Windy Gyle having climbed from Cocklawfoot on Bowmont Water and heads south-east down the upper reaches of the Coquet to Alwinton, a meeting place of several tracks across the hills. From Alwinton the Scottish cattle were herded south to Morpeth (N) and Newcastle (T), or to Corbridge (N) and on to the markets of Yorkshire. Its name comes from the once flourishing but now deserted village of Clennell, near Alwinton.

From the later Middle Ages to the coming of the railway cattle and sheep in large numbers were moved across country on well established routes, with inns and overnight pastures serving the needs of men and beasts. Usually the tracks were sufficiently wide to accommodate herds of up to 200 cattle, and flocks of more than 1,000 sheep, and stopping places were frequent. Progress would be little more than 12 miles (19.31km) a day and often less. Many of these routes are still visible on the remote hills, but elsewhere they are under modern roads and remembered only in field names and on the occasional inn sign.

Other drove roads crossed the western parts of the Cheviots to Gilsland (C) and then across the northern Pennines to long established markets at Appleby (61,C) and Brough (64,C). From Galloway, cattle were brought to Carlisle and to the once thriving market of Rosley, south-west of Carlisle, using the fords across the Solway Firth.

In the Lake District a network of local drove roads linked remote farms with the larger markets and the same roads were used, as elsewhere, by travellers and by packhorses, negotiating slopes impossible for wheeled vehicles. The drove road from Eskdale to Cockermouth is still traceable and can be followed on foot, and parts of others including 'Galwaithegate', the Galloway road, on the eastern edge of the Lakes, can also be pursued.

77

Corbridge, Vicar's Pele, Northumberland
Middle Ages

OS 87 NY 988644. Corbridge. 3 miles (4.8km) E of Hexham on A69

[A]

St Andrew's church is in the centre of Corbridge, immediately north of the market-place. Near the church, on the

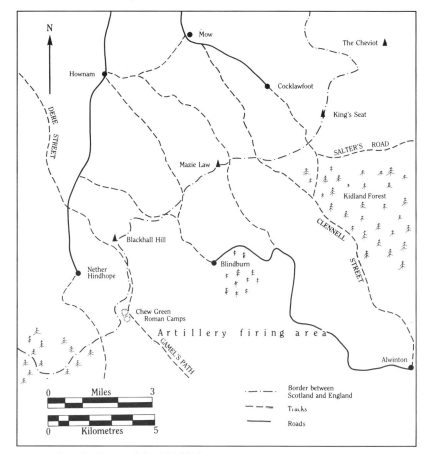

Drove roads in the Cheviots (after J T White). EH

south side of the churchyard, is the medieval priest's house, a 14th-century three-storeyed tower. The entrance is on the east side, unusually at ground floor level, and defended by a 'yett', a door reinforced with iron bars. The basement is vaulted and has two narrow loop holes as windows. Above this, reached by steps in the thickness of the wall, is the living room with a fireplace, garderobe (latrine) and sink. Over this is the bedchamber which may also have served as an oratory. There is a stone book shelf or lectern in one wall. At roof level, behind the battlements, is a wall-walk for use as a fighting platform.

That a miniature fortress was needed to protect the parish priest reflects the turbulence of the times. The northern counties were ravaged by Scottish raiders, especially after the English defeat at Bannockburn in 1314 and, in response, fortified towers were built to protect their owners and households. In a list of more than 100 castles in Northumberland in 1415, most are towers of this type, and there were many others in neighbouring counties and across the border. A large number still survive, often called 'peles' or 'pele towers', some still lived in, but many now in ruins.

Corbridge itself is at an important crossing of the Tyne. It was a royal burgh in Anglian times and, in the Middle Ages, a prosperous market centre with a charter granted by King John in 1201. Continuous prosperity is reflected in its substantial houses, several with 18th-century datestones. The market-cross was presented by the duke of Northumberland in 1814. Also in the market-place is a spring house with a pyramidal roof.

Much of St Andrew's church is 13th-century in date. Its west tower, however, is older and of exceptional interest. The lower part is the porch of an early monastic church which may have been founded in the 7th century and was certainly in existence by 786. Like the similar sequence at Monkwearmouth (29,T) it was originally of one or two storeys, but later heightened, possibly in the 11th century, and made into a tower with a belfry in its top stage. Many of the stones are Roman and especially those of

Corbridge vicar's pele. EH

the arch in its east wall, leading into the nave. Presumably they came from Corstopitum, a quarter of a mile (0.5km) to the west. Above the arches of the north arcade are parts of two early windows, and other evidence of an early church has been found below the floor.

78

Farmhouses and Farm Buildings

There are few farmhouses and farm buildings in the northern counties

earlier than 1650. The humbler buildings of earlier times were poorly built, like the 'sad little hutts made up of drye walls, only stones piled together', seen by Celia Fiennes during her northern journey of 1698. But in the second half of the 17th century a surge of new building took place, attested by the datestones that still survive above many doorways.

Of particular interest are the farmhouses, sometimes called 'states-mens' houses', which are characteristic of the Lake District. In a typical plan the doorway leads into a passage, the 'hallan', which runs from front to back and has

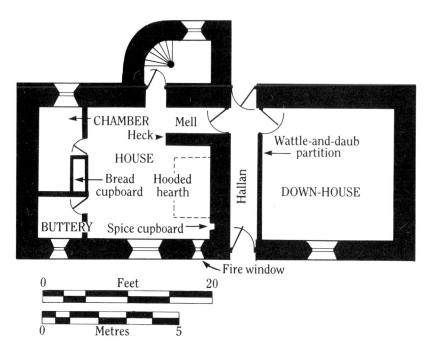

Plan of a statesman's house (after W Rollinson). EH

doorways at each end. The combined living room and kitchen is on one side of the 'hallan', and on the other is the 'down-house', often unceiled and used for washing, brewing, and general storage.

From the 'hallan', a shorter passage, the 'mell', leads into the living room, the wall of the passage protecting the fireplace from draughts. Above the hearth is a large canopy or hood made of lath and plaster which narrows to a flue as it passes through the loft above. Opposite the hearth is the bread cupboard, elaborately carved and built into a partition which separates the bedchamber and buttery from the living room. The loft above, the sleeping place of the children and servants, is open to the roof.

In other arrangements, although the plan of the living quarters remains the same, the 'down-house' is omitted and replaced by a cow-byre, giving a continuous range of house and farm buildings still frequently encountered among the smaller upland farms. Some

see it as a vestigial form of the ancient 'long-house', sheltering men and beasts under one roof.

Increasing prosperity and higher living standards brought radical changes in house plans. Traditional arrangements were modified and the transformation from the 'statesman' plan to a more spacious style of living is clearly demonstrated at the farmhouse of the Browne family at Townend, Troutbeck (81,C), which is now in the ownership of the National Trust and open to the public.

Larger and more symmetrical houses were built from the later years of the 18th century onwards, with rooms front and back and with more bedrooms on the upper floor. They are scattered throughout the area but are particularly prominent in the Eden valley and in the eastern parts of Northumberland, often secluded and partly hidden by the surrounding farm buildings, and invariably of quiet and satisfying design.

A number of cruck-built barns survive, but more characteristic of the

area are the field barns or 'field-houses' of the Pennine valleys and, to a lesser extent, of the Lake District, and also 'bank-barns'. Larger than the field barns, like them they are built to take advantage of the sloping ground, with direct access to both floors. At the upper level is a threshing floor with storage bays on either side, and at ground level are cow-byre, stable and cartshed. Their greatest concentration is in the Lake District and they are seldom found elsewhere. The barn at Townend is of this type.

Wooden galleries sheltered by extended eaves are found attached to both farmhouses and farm buildings. Although popularly associated with spinning, they may have served primarily as storage and drying places as well as giving convenient access to the upper floor. Generally they are on the north and east sides of the buildings rather than on the south and west.

With the extensive enclosure of land in the 18th and 19th centuries came larger farms newly built away from established villages, and in the case of estate farms, such as those of east Northumberland especially, providing purpose built cottages for their farm labourers. The larger farms often adopted steam power and, although the engines rarely survive, the chimneys of their engine-houses are tell-tale evidence. An excellent example of a farm lay-out of the 1790s with a 19th-century engine house is at the North of England Open Air Museum at Beamish (97,D).

79
Glencoynedale Shieling, Cumbria
Middle Ages or later

OS 90 NY 376185. Patterdale.
2 miles (3.2km) NW of Patterdale on A592, then by footpath S of car park
[D]

In 1599 William Camden visited Cumberland and Hadrian's Wall and observed the transhumance being practiced in the area. He described, in

Britannia (1610 edn), 'the ancient Nomades, a martiall kinde of men, who from the moneth of Aprill unto August, lye out scattering and summering (as they tearme it) with their cattell in little cottages here and there which they call Sheales and Shealings.'

'Shiel' is Norse for a summer pasture and the migration of herdsmen with their families and their stock from winter settlements to summer grazing in the hills was taking place in the Lake District in the 10th and 11th centuries. It was widespread in the northern counties throughout the Middle Ages and continued in parts of the North well into the 17th century. An echo of the system, without the movement of people, survives in the summer grazing of stints on the high moors.

A 'shieling' is the cottage used by the herdsman and his family. Some were built of turf, others of drystone walling with turf on the roof. Generally they were rectangular in plan and the larger ones were subdivided into two, and occasionally into three, rooms. Windows were rare, and although there were hearths, no chimney has been found in any of the surviving examples. Often they were clustered together in groups, near a stream.

Not one has survived complete, but their ruins can be found in remote parts of the hills. A survey by RCHME (*Shielings and Bastles*, HMSO, 1970) recorded 136 shielings in selected parts of Cumbria and Northumberland, some surviving only as levelled platforms in the ground and others with partial and tumbled walls. To find them usually involves strenuous walking on the high moors, which should only be attempted with proper precautions and with due regard to the use and ownership of the surrounding land. Not all the temporary dwellings were used by herdsmen. A few were miners' huts, virtually indistinguishable in structure from those that went with summer pasturing.

80

Newton Arlosh, St John's Church, Cumbria
Middle Ages

OS 85 NY 198552. Newton Arlosh. On B5307 15 miles (24km) W of Carlisle

[C]

St John's Church, Newton Arlosh, was built about 1305 by the monks of Holme Cultram abbey as the parish church of a 'new town', replacing the village of Skinburness overwhelmed by the sea. Much of the church was rebuilt in the 19th century, but its south wall and west tower are medieval; the tower a grim,

Glencoynedale shieling above Ullswater. RCHME

St John's church, Newton Arlosh.
TOM HOUGHTON

unornamented structure with few windows and no external entrance. Indeed, it was built for defence, its ground floor vaulted and with access at first floor level from inside the church, probably by way of a removeable ladder. It is one of a number in the Border counties where the turmoil of the later Middle Ages and the threat of attack led to the church tower being made a refuge for the priest and others. In Cumbria, the churches at Burgh by Sands and Great Salkeld have fortified west towers. In Northumberland, Embleton church and St Anne's, Ancroft have fortified towers.

Monasteries, too, made provision for defence. At Lanercost Priory (39,C) a fortified tower was added to the west range, and at Lindisfarne Priory on Holy Island (38,N) high defensive walls were built in the early 14th century and a barbican added to the inner gateway. At Tynemouth (59,T) a powerful new gatehouse was built to increase the defences of the castle and protect the priory sheltering within its walls. Neither priest nor peasant was immune from attack during this period.

81

Townend, Cumbria
17th century and later

OS 90 NY 407020. Troutbeck. Off A592 at S end of Troutbeck village by minor road
[A] NT

There are records of Brownes at Townend in the early part of the 16th century and their tenure of the property may have begun even earlier. It remained with the family until 1944, a span of more than four centuries. Externally the house is a typical Lakeland building with rendered and whitewashed walls, slated roofs, and the large round chimneys often found where the local building material is the hard, unyielding, carboniferous limestone. Internally the oldest part, dating from the late 16th or early 17th century, is the present living room, with the kitchen added about 1623 on the occasion of the marriage of George Browne with Susannah Rawlinson of Grizedale Hall. Increasing prosperity brought more changes. The north wing was built later in the 17th century to provide a new staircase, a parlour and a bedroom, and the west wing was added in 1739.

Some modernisation in the form of fireplace surrounds and kitchen equipment took place in the 19th century, but these have not affected its essential character. It remains a remarkably complete example of a well-to-do yeoman farmer's house, together with its fittings, which include several pieces of furniture carved by members of the family. Across the road is a bank barn with a gallery built in 1666.

82

Wasdale Head Packhorse Bridge, Cumbria
17th or 18th century

OS 89 NY 187090. Wasdale. A595 to Gosforth, then by minor road through Nether Wasdale and by side of West Water to Wasdale Head
[C]

Before the turnpike roads of the 18th century, one of the principal means of moving goods, especially in the uplands, was the packhorse. Celia Fiennes, travelling from Kendal to Bowness in 1698 (*Journeys*), commented on the local use of 'horses on which they have a sort of pannyers some close some open that they strew full of hay turff and lime and dung and every thing they would use.' For bulk transport, trains of ten to twenty or more sturdy ponies, usually Galloways, each carrying 2cwts in panniers strapped to wooden pack saddles, criss-crossed the country carrying wool, cloth, salt, slate, coal, lead ore and lead, from distant farms, mines, mills, and coastal saltpans to local markets, and to the larger towns. It was slow but reliable. From Kendal, the

Townend farmhouse, Troutbeck. JOHN BETHELL

Wasdale Head packhorse bridge. J ALLAN CASH

hub of several packhorse trains, the journey to London took more than two weeks, averaging 15 miles (24.14km) a day.

Bridges were needed for the heavily laden animals when river crossings were difficult. The earliest, over the smaller streams in the Lake District, were probably made of wooden planks supported on logs. Stone piers replaced the logs and, where the traffic warranted it, stone arches were built spanning the streams. Typically they are narrow and have low parapets to give clearance for the side panniers. They are difficult to date. Those in the Lake District are probably not earlier than the 17th century.

83

Wetheriggs Pottery, Cumbria
19th century

OS 90 NY 555264. Clifton. 3 miles (4.8km) SE of Penrith, on minor road from A6

[A]

The pottery was built in 1855 for the Brougham Hall estate by a Mr Binings. It consists of a large, brick-built 'beehive' kiln 20ft (6 m) high with eight firemouths round its base. Surrounding the kiln is a covered working area so that externally the chimney of the kiln emerges from a series of pent roofs. Its appetite for fuel was prodigious. Six tons of coal were needed to raise the temperature to 1,100° centigrade over a period of thirty-six hours, and cooling took a further two to three days. Clay was obtained from a pit in the grounds and worked by steam-driven machinery, most of which survives.

Production continued until the 1950s, the pottery making domestic ware for kitchens and dairies, and bricks, tiles and drainpipes for agricultural and building uses. It was revived in the 1970s, modernised, and is still a working pottery but using more modern machinery and kilns. The 19th-century kiln has been preserved and is on display and visitors are able to see both the Victorian equipment and

modern pottery making. A shop sells Wetheriggs pottery which is based on traditional patterns.

84

Yanwath Hall, Cumbria
Middle Ages and later

OS 90 NY 508282. Penrith. 1½ miles (2.4km) SW of Penrith on B5320

[D]

Yanwath Hall is a fortified medieval house, altered in the 16th century but without major changes since and therefore an excellent example of its type. It has three ranges of buildings, but only one is visible from the nearby road. It is the earliest of the three, dating from the 14th century, and has a battlemented tower at its west end. Within the main part of the range is a great hall, once open to the roof, with a screens passage and, beyond the

passage, a kitchen. The tower is entered from the hall and has one chamber on each floor with a newel staircase in one corner giving access to the upper chambers and the roof. The chamber at ground floor level has a stone vault.

In the early part of the 14th century, Yanwath was owned by John de Sutton. Towards the end of the century it was acquired by the Threlkeld family, who rebuilt part and added the bay window on the south side of the hall. In the 16th century it was in the possession of the Dudleys. In the later part of the century larger windows were put into the upper chambers of the tower and their interiors refitted, and an intermediate floor inserted in the great hall, reducing it in size and making additional rooms above. In 1671 the property passed to the Lowthers and from that time onwards it has been used as a farm, escaping the attentions of 18th and 19th-century improvers.

It will be apparent even from a distant view that Yanwath was only partly fortified. Whereas properties

Wetheriggs Pottery. WETHERIGGS COUNTRY POTTERY

Yanwath Hall. RCHME

nearer the border had all their accommodation securely contained within their towers, at Yanwath the great hall and kitchen are not defended. Nor is it an isolated example. There are similar, partly-fortified houses at Blencow and Catterlen north-east of Penrith, and others at Beetham and Kentmere, near Kendal. At Clifton, 2.5 miles (4km) south of Penrith, a tower survives in isolation, but this is deceptive: it once had additional living quarters, since destroyed.

Yanwath is not normally open to the public, but it is an attractive and interesting building and even a distant examination is rewarding. The Clifton tower is in the care of English Heritage.

8

Country Houses and Gardens

The story of the great houses of the North begins with feudal strongholds. Several were adapted to meet new needs, their ancient walls retained but their interiors entirely renewed. This happened, for example, at Alnwick (47,N), Raby (58,D), Lumley (55,D) and Naworth (56,C). Others, with fortified towers, were given new additions, like **Belsay** (86,N), Chipchase (N) and **Hutton-in-the-Forest** (90,C). So there is a fascinating continuity in many of these buildings. Their origins lie in the Middle Ages but they speak also of Jacobean improvements, of Georgian expansion, and of Victorian opulence. Even **Wallington** (96,N) and **Dalemain** (88,C), serenely Georgian on the outside, have older parts hidden in the basement or tucked away in lesser ranges at the rear.

Without exception they are built of stone, occasionally of hard rubble, more often of beautifully cut sandstone, pink or pinkish-grey on the west side of the country, **Holker** (89,C) and Dalemain, and brown or greyish-brown on the east, ranging from the sombre tones of Alnwick and **Seaton Delaval** (94,N) to the biscuit-coloured ashlar of Belsay and Wallington.

The change from fortress to gentleman's residence is well illustrated at **Levens** (91,C), where the medieval tower and hall were transformed into an Elizabethan house. Also at **Sizergh** (95,C), enlarged and remodelled in the same period, except for its tower, a grim reminder of the house's medieval origins. However, the best example of the change from war to peace is at Belsay, where in 1614 a Jacobean house was built against the formidable 14th-century tower, expressing in stone the ending of centuries of Border warfare. Similar transformations took place at Chipchase, where the Jacobean range was added in 1621, and at Chillingham (N), which was remodelled about 1630. (Neither of these houses is open to the public.)

Country house architecture in the North never entirely lost its military undertones. Sir John Vanbrugh's stupendous house at Seaton Delaval, designed for Admiral Delaval, has the character of a medieval keep, while long-established families continued to live in their castles: Percys and their successors at Alnwick, Howards at Naworth, and Vanes at Raby. They improved the interiors, and rebuilt parts of the medieval fabric, but the baronial element remained alive and strong. Even at the end of the 19th century, Lord Armstrong, builder of **Cragside** (87,N) was drawn to the ancient stronghold of Bamburgh (48,N), and renewed its interior. More recently still, in the early years of this century, the artillery fort on Holy Island (38,N) attracted Edward Hudson to make an occasional residence within its gun emplacements, using the skills of Edwin Lutyens to transform the barrack rooms and magazines into places of architectural magic and delight.

Of course some houses entirely escaped the military embrace. **Rokeby Park** (93,D) is a beautiful Palladian mansion of the early 18th century, and Belford Hall (N) and Bywell Hall (N), both the work of the architect James Paine and slightly later, are completely classical. Dalemain and Wallington, too, although with earlier origins, are essentially classical and in the case of Wallington with an exceptionally rich interior. Later in date and Grecian in style is Belsay Hall, third in date of the trio of buildings at this extraordinarily interesting site. The new house built by Sir Charles Monck between 1810 and 1817 is in the same park as the medieval tower and Jacobean house, but entirely separate and not even within view. The tower, once so mighty, became a picturesque feature in the grounds. Rokeby, Dalemain, Wallington and Belsay are regularly open to visitors; Belford Hall and Bywell Hall are not open to the public.

Of other 19th-century buildings, Lowther Castle (C) was designed by Robert Smirke for the earl of Lonsdale

Cragside. AFK

and built between 1806 and 1811. It is a castellated mansion, now without roofs, floors or windows, but princely in scale and, even in ruin, engagingly romantic. Princely, too, are the 19th-century interiors of Alnwick and Raby. It was the age of great estates and also of great industrial wealth, best seen at Cragside, the creation of Lord Armstrong, scientist, inventor and industrialist. But perhaps the most extravagant of all these great buildings is the country mansion built in the form of a French chateau by John Bowes, and now the Bowes Museum, Barnard Castle (62,D). Seen from a distance its roofs and towers glitter in the sun 'like a stretch of the Louvre'; inappropriate perhaps, but magnificent.

85

Belle Isle, Cumbria
18th century

OS 97 SD 393965. Windermere. Can be glimpsed from lakeside, and from lake steamers

[D]

Belle Isle is an island of 38 acres (15.38ha) in the middle of Lake

Belle Isle. CL

Belsay Hall. EH

Windermere. It contains an extraordinary and very attractive house, circular in plan and with a domed roof. It was built for a Mr English in 1774 to the design of the architect John Plaw and is the first of its type in England. A larger, grander version is Ickworth, Suffolk, begun in 1791. The entrance has a giant portico with Ionic columns and, flanking the doorway, niches containing marble statues of Autumn and Spring. Inside, the staircase takes up the central part of the house rising the full height, and is lit from above by windows in the cupola which, ingeniously, also has chimney flues built into its walls. The rooms are decorated in neo-classical style.

The house was bought, still unfinished, in 1781 by Isabella Curwen. She and her husband completed the building and landscaped the grounds to the plan of Thomas White, a follower of the great 'Capability' Brown. The house was used primarily as a summer residence and, although some regarded it as an unwelcome intrusion, others followed its example with enthusiasm, building picturesque villas of great variety on lakeside properties.

86

Belsay Hall and Castle, Northumberland
Middle Ages, 17th and 19th centuries

OS 88 NZ 088785. Belsay. 14 miles (22.5km) NW of Newcastle on A696

[A] EH

Belsay Hall was built by Sir Charles Monck in the early part of the 19th century. The foundations were started in 1807 and it was ready for occupation in 1817. It has been described as the most perfect Greek Revival house in England.

Sir Charles was born in 1779, the son of Sir William Middleton of Belsay. In 1799 he changed his name to Monck for purposes of inheritance. He married in 1804 and, after a European tour which included a year in Athens studying classical Greek architecture, he returned to England with his wife in 1806, resolved to build 'in the manner of the Greeks'. He may have obtained practical help from the Newcastle architect John Dobson, then at the beginning of his career, but the design is his own, inspired by his studies in Athens and influenced also by neo-classical buildings he had seen in Berlin.

It is a severe, uncompromising building, exactly 100ft square (929 square m), with its principal doorway treated like the entrance to a Greek temple and dwarfed by two giant Doric columns. At the centre of the house is a two-storeyed hall surrounded by two tiers of columns and with an overhead lantern. Around the hall are the principal rooms, regrettably kept entirely bare. Photographs of the rooms when they were still in use and furnished are included in an exhibition in the stables.

From the gardens near the house paths lead to the quarry gardens, landscaped and planted by Sir Charles and extended by his successor, Sir Arthur Middleton, later in the century. They used the quarry from which stone was taken to build the house and planted it with evergreens and rare shrubs to make it one of the most beautiful informal gardens in Britian.

Beyond the quarry is Belsay Castle, a 14th-century tower house with the remains of a Jacobean wing attached to one side. The tower was repaired and partially restored in the 19th century and, consequently, is more accessible than most. It has a kitchen on the ground floor, a hall on the first floor, and chamber above, with smaller chambers in adjacent parts. It is one of the many fortified towers built in the border counties in the later Middle Ages when raid and counter-raid made the area lawless and insecure, but larger, and more sophisticated in plan than most. The contrast between warlike tower and Jacobean house with its large windows and easy access could not provide a better illustration of the change to more peaceful times in the turbulent history of the Border counties.

87

Cragside, Northumberland
19th century

OS 81 NU 073022. Rothbury. Entrance at Debdon Gate 1 mile (1.6km) N of Rothbury on B6341

[A] NT

Cragside began as a modest-sized house built by Sir William Armstrong on 20 acres (8.09ha) of land bought in 1863. It was intended for occasional summer use, as a change from Newcastle where Armstrong had his principal house, at Jesmond Dene, and his engineering and armaments works. The site when purchased was a bare and rocky hillside above Debdon Burn, and the first house was a rather plain mid-Victorian villa.

Six years later it was decided to expand. In 1869 Richard Norman Shaw was commissioned to transform the summer retreat into a country mansion and Armstrong, purchasing more land and planting it with several million trees, turned the bleak hillside into a forest. He made carriageways and paths, formed lakes and waterways, and,

Cragside. The drawing-room. RCHME

harnessing the streams, brought electricity and hydraulic power to drive the kitchen machinery and lifts. Cragside was described at the time as 'the palace of a modern magician.' It was the world's first private house to be lit by hydro-electricity, initially by arc lamps and later by incandescent bulbs.

The architecture, too, is extraordinary. In a sense it reflects the medieval fortresses of Northumberland, towered and turreted, but it is a romantic castle not a medieval replica, and its details are an odd medley of stone walls, half-timbering, gothic arches and 'Tudor' windows. The house grew by a series of additions, retaining the original building and extending it horizontally and vertically. Shaw was involved until 1884 but work continued until Sir William, then Lord, Armstrong's death in 1900.

Many of the rooms are quite small. The principal interiors are the library and dining-room, decorated in a comfortable 'Old English' style with beamed ceilings and panelled walls, and a much grander drawing-room, one of Shaw's last works at Cragside. This has an overpoweringly large chimneypiece made of Italian marbles and designed by W R Lethaby. But Cragside is more than just an unusually complete late Victorian building. House and grounds reflect the character of their owner, a remarkable scientist and engineer. He inspired and controlled all that was done and it is this that gives Cragside its unique interest.

88

Dalemain, Cumbria
18th century, with earlier parts

OS 90 NY 478269. Near Penrith. 3 miles (4.8km) SW of Penrith on A592

[A]

Cumbria has few Georgian mansions. Dalemain is probably the best. In its present form it is the work of Edward Hasell who built the east range and the side elevations about the middle of the

18th century, employing an architect whose name is not known. Edward's father, Sir Edward Hasell, bought the estate in 1680. He was the steward of the redoubtable Lady Anne Clifford, some of whose achievements are recorded in the entry on Brougham castle (50,C).

But, as elsewhere, the history of the house begins in the Middle Ages with a pele tower and hall, which was improved and extended in the 16th century. These parts are in the west range, on the far side of the inner courtyard from the Georgian apartments. The Old Hall, Oak Room and Fretwork Room, which has an interesting ribbed plaster ceiling, belong to these earlier periods.

The Georgian rooms include one drawing-room decorated with a Chinese hand-painted wallpaper bought for the house about 1750 and, in the same room, an intricately carved rococo-style wooden chimneypiece. A second drawing-room is entirely panelled in oak, and in the entrance hall there is an elegant, open staircase rising through two storeys. The dining-room dates from 1785.

Dalemain. CL

In the outer courtyard are farm buildings which include a high barn, a threshing barn, coach houses and stables for carriage horses. The Westmorland and Cumberland Yeomanry Museum is in part of the pele tower in the house.

89

Holker Hall, Cumbria
17th century and later

OS 96 SD 359774. Cartmel. Between Kendal and Ulverston on A590 and B5277 or B5278
[A]

Holker began modestly as a 17th-century house built by George Preston, a local landowner and a liberal benefactor of Cartmel priory (35,C). From the Prestons it passed by marriage at the end of the 17th century to the Lowthers, and in 1756 to the Cavendishes, increasing in size as the result of several building campaigns. These began in the 1720s and ended in 1840 when the exterior was entirely remodelled by the architect George Webster of Kendal. The Old Wing retains work of these earlier periods and has a facade dating from 1840. In 1871 there was a devastating fire. The west wing was destroyed, and promptly rebuilt on a grander scale by William Cavendish, 7th duke of Devonshire, employing Paley and Austin of Lancaster as architects. The New Wing is a bold, confident work, based on Elizabethan models, but unmistakeably Victorian in character.

Inside there is a succession of very large, spacious rooms including a 16th-century-style long gallery and a scheme of decoration which uses an Elizabethan vocabulary for plasterwork and panelling. The furniture is mainly 18th and 19th-century, some brought from Chatsworth to make good the losses suffered in the fire. From Chatsworth, too, is part of the library, which includes books of the 18th-century scientist, Henry Cavendish.

Near the house are attractive formal gardens, while outbuildings house the Lakeland Motor Museum and an exhibition of Lakeland life and industry.

Holker Hall. CL

90

Hutton-in-the-Forest, Cumbria
Middle Ages and later

OS 90 NY 460358. Skelton near Penrith. 5 miles (8km) NW of Penrith by M6 or A6 then B5305
[A]

The 'forest' is the royal forest of Inglewood which lay between Penrith and Carlisle west of the River Eden. In the Middle Ages the lord of the manor of Hutton was one of three principal subforesters whose duties were to preserve the game and maintain the forest laws.

Parts of the house are still recognisably medieval, especially the north tower which has a vaulted ground floor chamber, now the entrance hall, but first impressions are coloured by the huge south tower, mainly 19th-century, and the central part of the facade, which was built in the 1680s. The two are startlingly different. The one dark and gothic; the other light and baroque. On the right-hand side of the entrance court (north) is a building of the mid-17th century which has a long gallery on its upper floor and, below this, a *loggia*, originally open but now with glazed windows. An 18th-century engraving shows a balancing range on the south side of the courtyard, but this was never built.

The interior owes much to an extensive campaign of remodelling and rebuilding by the architect Anthony Salvin, who was working here in the 1820s, and again in the 1860s and 1880s. However, there is a splendid late 17th-century staircase, carved with foliage

Hutton-in-the-Forest. CL

and cherubs, moved to its present position in the 19th century, and for those interested in the 'Arts and Crafts' movement, there are William Morris furnishings in one of the bedrooms.

Hutton was bought by Sir Richard Fletcher of Cockermouth in 1605. It came to the Vanes by inheritance in 1735 and has remained with the family to this day. There is an excellent series of family portraits, principally in the long gallery. North of the house is a walled garden dating from the 1730s, and there is an attractive woodland walk for which a leaflet is available. On the edge of the park is a 17th-century dovecote.

91

Levens Hall, Cumbria
Mainly 16th and 17th centuries

OS 97 SD 496851. Levens near Kendal. 5 miles (8km) S of Kendal on A6, or join A6 at junction 36 of M6 motorway

[A]

The most famous feature of Levens is its topiary garden. It was laid out for the then owner, James Grahme, about 1700

by a French garden designer, Guillaume Beaumont. His portrait is in the house with the inscription, 'Gardener to King James II and Col. James Grahme. He laid out the Gardens at Hampton Court Palace and at Levens.'

The house is older. It began, as did many country houses in this area, with a medieval pele tower and hall, and was enlarged and remodelled by James Bellingham, whose father bought the property in 1562. James Bellingham gained possession about 1580 and transformed it into an Elizabethan house with interiors typical of the period. There is Elizabethan plasterwork

Levens Hall. BOYS SYNDICATION

and panelling in the great hall, drawing-room, small drawing-room, and dining-room, and two splendid two-tier chimney pieces, one dated 1586 and one 1595. Originally there was a long gallery over the hall but this is now divided into smaller rooms.

In 1688 Levens was sold to Colonel James Grahme, the last Bellingham owner having gambled his way into debt. Grahme installed a fine staircase leading from the great hall, built a new wing for domestic offices, with a brewhouse, and laid out the gardens. The Cordova leather wall-hangings in the dining-room are his, and so are the superb Charles II dining chairs. Steam enthusiasts will find a display of working models in the brewhouse, as well as a number of full-size steam engines.

92

Muncaster Castle, Cumbria
Middle Ages and later

OS 96 SD 103964. Ravenglass. On A595 1 mile (1.6km) E of Ravenglass
[A]

One of the two towers on Muncaster's west front is a 14th-century pele tower; the other is the work of the architect Anthony Salvin in the 1860s, commissioned by the 4th Lord Muncaster. There is little medieval work surviving in the castle other than the tower, which has a tunnel-vault at ground level, the hallmark of its type. Salvin, on the other hand, is very much

in evidence, but not stridently so. His work is restrained and scholarly, and a pleasure to see.

The best interiors are the great hall and dining-room, in baronial style, a very elegant classical drawing-room with coved ceiling and marble fireplace, and the octagonal library which rises through two storeys to a ribbed ceiling. The library was begun in the 1780s but modified by Salvin; it stands on the site of the medieval kitchens. Elsewhere in the house are fittings and furniture of 16th-century date (West, King's and Tapestry rooms), some imported from other houses; there is a good collection of family portraits, and the 'Luck of Muncaster', an enamelled glass bowl, reputedly given by Henry VI in gratitude for shelter in time of need. An octagonal tower in the grounds marks the place where the king was found, the story goes. Among the portraits is one of Thomas Skelton, 'the last Fool of Muncaster'. The castle grounds are famed for their planting and for the views of Eskdale and the hills of central Lakeland.

Muncaster mill, 1 mile (1.5km) to the north-west, has medieval origins, but the present building dates from c.1700. Closed in 1961, it has been

restored and is again a working corn mill powered by an overshot waterwheel.

93

Rokeby Park, County Durham
18th century

OS 92 NZ 083143. Greta Bridge. 3 miles (4.8km) SE of Barnard Castle by minor road, or by A66 to Greta Bridge
[A]

Rokeby was designed by Sir Thomas Robinson who inherited the property in 1720. Robinson was an accomplished amateur architect with an enthusiasm for Palladian architecture, a taste he shared with his friend and adviser, Lord Burlington. The old house was discarded and to replace it Robinson built an Italianate villa using as his model the work of the 16th-century architect Andrea Palladio. It consists of a compact, beautifully proportioned, central block with a pyramidal roof, flanked by smaller blocks with similar roofs but set further back. Flanking these, and set even further back, are

Muncaster Castle, CL

later pavilions. Originally there was complete symmetry. Later alterations put extra storeys on the eastern wings.

Entry now is at ground floor level on the south side into a low columned hall with family rooms – library and dining-room – on either side. The state rooms are on the floor above and originally there was direct access from an outside staircase. The grandest room is the saloon, occupying much of the upper floor and rising through two storeys. It was here that the most splendid of the family's possessions was hung, the 'Rokeby Venus', painted by Velasquez and acquired in 1813. It is now in the National Gallery, London, replaced in the house by a copy painted in 1906. Other rooms next to the saloon have late 18th-century plasterwork and fittings, and the decoration of the state dining-room in the west wing is also of this period and possibly by the architect, Carr of York. The house was sold by Sir Thomas in 1769 to J S Morritt who, as well as these alterations, built Rokeby church in 1778, and the famous bridge over the River Greta in 1773. It was designed by Carr of York. Morritt was succeeded by his son, J B S Morritt, a patron of the arts, who invited Sir Walter Scott to stay at the hall and also the painter John Sell Cotman. Scott dedicated his epic poem *Rokeby*, published in 1813, to Morritt, and among several paintings by Cotman of the River Greta and its surroundings is one of his best known works *Greta Bridge*, painted in 1807.

Rokeby Park. EDDIE RYLE-HODGES

94

Seaton Delaval Hall, Northumberland
18th century

OS 88 NZ 322766. Seaton Delaval.
9 miles (14.5km) NE of Newcastle
by A189 and A190

[A]

The setting of the house is disappointing
and its central building was gutted by
fire in 1822, losing much of the interior.
Nevertheless, Seaton Delaval is one of
the grandest buildings in England and
one of the most dramatic. It was
designed for Admiral George Delaval by
Sir John Vanbrugh, soldier, playwright,
Clarenceux King of Arms, and, at a later
stage in his life, architect. The first
house he designed was Castle Howard in
Yorkshire, followed shortly afterwards
by Blenheim Palace in Oxfordshire for
the duke and duchess of Marlborough.
He was appointed Comptroller of the
Royal Works in 1702, becoming a
colleague of Sir Christopher Wren and
virtually his deputy. Seaton Delaval is
one of his last designs. It was built
between 1718 and 1728. Neither owner
nor architect lived to see its completion.

The principal apartments are in the
central block which rises up like a
medieval keep, dark and menacing.
Flanking this, and at right angles to the
central block, are east and west ranges,
lower and more soberly treated, which
enclose the entrance court. The east
range housed the stables. In the west
were the kitchens, now converted into a
separate house. Both ranges were
arcaded at ground level, the arcades
ending in pavilions which mark the
entrance and, in Vanbrugh's design, are
shown linked together by a wall and
central gateway. The north front of the
central block has giant Tuscan columns
flanking the entrance; the garden side,
facing south, has a portico with fluted
Ionic columns.

Though gutted, the central block is
roofed and its windows are framed and
glazed. Internally, although badly
damaged, sufficient remains of the great
hall to see its arrangement and detail. It

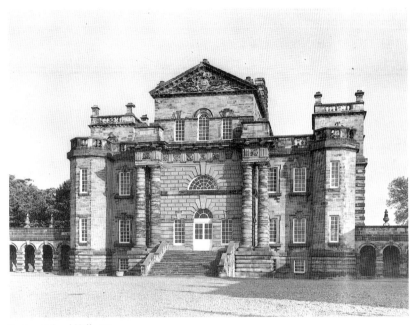

Seaton Delaval Hall. AFK

rises through two storeys with a gallery
at the inner end. The lower walls are
treated with blind arcading and the
upper parts with niches filled with
statues. Vaulted corridors lead to
staircases in the side towers. Beyond the
hall the south front of the house was
entirely taken up by the saloon which
was divided into three parts by screens of
Corinthian columns.

Vanbrugh's buildings belong to the
brief flowering of an English baroque
style. They are monumental, theatrical,
and majestic. However, their influence
was short lived. Within a generation
architectural taste turned to the
Palladianism of Lord Burlington and his
associates, and Vanbrugh's works were
despised. Elsewhere in the North he
provided designs for the town hall at
Morpeth (N), renewed and altered after a
fire in the 19th century. He was
responsible for alterations at Lumley
Castle (55,D) and very probably, was
associated with the design of
Ravensdowne Barracks in Berwick
(49,N). His works are few in number but
bear the unmistakeable stamp of his
genius and, for those who enjoy
powerful and dramatic buildings, are
worth a pilgrimage.

In the grounds south-east of the
house is a mausoleum, built in 1766,
and within easy reach is St Mary's
church, which has interesting Norman
work. The harbour at Seaton Sluice (NY
338768) was developed by the Delavals
in the 17th century to export coal and
salt. The bold cut through the rock to
the sea was made in the 1760s to provide
a new entrance and a deep-water dock.

95

Sizergh Castle, Cumbria
Middle Ages and later

OS 97 SD 498879. Near Kendal. On
A6 3½ miles (5.6km) S of Kendal

[A] NT

Sizergh's medieval origins are
immediately apparent. At its south-west
corner stands a massive tower 60ft (18
m) high, with turrets rising higher.
Typically, it is vaulted at ground level as
a defence against fire. But Sizergh is a
fortified house rather than a castle. Next
to the tower was a hall and, beyond the
hall, possibly a second, smaller tower. A
second tower in this position is unusual,

but not unknown. Bencow Hall and Askerton Castle are other Cumbrian houses with similar plans.

In the 16th century Sizergh was enlarged and remodelled. The two long ranges flanking the entrance court are Elizabethan, and both hall and tower were refitted at this time. They possess sumptuous 16th-century panelling and a remarkable series of chimneypieces with carved overmantels, many of them dated. At the top of the tower is the Inlaid Room which has an ornate plaster ceiling with coats of arms and heraldic beasts. The bed, which is dated 1568, was sold in 1896 but returned on loan by the Victoria and Albert Museum. The museum still retains the original panelling from this room, which is a pity. Among the furniture are some fine 16th-century chairs and benches. The house was remodelled again in the 18th century, when sash windows were introduced in the hall range, and the great hall made into an 18th-century drawing-room.

Sizergh has been in Strickland ownership since the 13th century. In the 14th century a Strickland daughter married Robert de Wessingham of Warton, near Carnforth, and from this marriage is descended George

Sizergh Castle, AFK

Washington, first President of the United States (see 115,T). A Strickland fought at Agincourt and, two centuries later, Stricklands were on the side of the Royalists in the Civil War, suffering penalties as a result. Sizergh remained with the family until 1950 when the estate was given to the National Trust.

96
Wallington Hall, Northumberland
18th century

OS 81 NZ 029842. Cambo. 11 miles (17.6km) W of Morpeth on B6343, or A696 from Newcastle

[A] NT

Wallington was built by Sir William Blackett of Newcastle whose fortune came from coal-mining and shipping. He purchased the estate in 1688, pulled down the old building of the Fenwicks, and built a courtyard house whose shape and dimensions are reflected in the present building. However, little survives of Sir William's house. Appearance and interior decoration of present day Wallington are mainly the work of his grandson, Sir Walter Calverley Blackett (1728–1777), who employed the architect Daniel Garrett to refashion the house in a more up-to-date style. There were major internal changes including a fine staircase, and new interiors richly decorated with rococo plasterwork. This was modelled by a team of Italian *stuccatori* working at Wallington between 1740 and 1742. For the plasterwork of the saloon they were

Wallington Hall. AFK

paid £44/19/4, and for the plasterwork of the dining room, £23/19/6. The marble fireplaces and the woodwork are of equally high quality.

In 1777 Wallington was inherited by Sir John Trevelyan. In the 19th century the courtyard was roofed-in to make a two-storeyed central hall surrounded by two tiers of arcades and with a high coved ceiling. The architect was John Dobson and the historical scenes were painted by William Bell Scott, with other decoration provided by Pauline Trevelyan and her friends, including John Ruskin. The house was owned by the Trevelyans until 1941 when, together with the estate, it was given to the National Trust.

The stable court has a handsome north range with a clock tower and cupola, which is probably the work of Daniel Garrett. The gardens were developed from the 1730s onwards, with some architectural work by Garrett in 1740. In the 1760s another part of the estate at Rothley Lake, was landscaped by 'Capability' Brown. The bridge over the Wansbeck south of the house is by James Paine and was built in 1760.

To the north of Wallington, Cambo village has 18th and 19th-century estate cottages and a medieval pele tower. 'Capability' Brown, born Lancelot Brown in Kirkharle, about a mile and a half (2.5km) south-west of Wallington, went to the village school in Cambo.

9

Industry and Transport

Industrial activity is not a modern phenomenon. Iron was being worked in antiquity, and under the Romans lead mining in the Alston area was extensive and well organised. Coal was being exported from the Tyne basin in the later Middle Ages and the remains of primitive iron-smelting bloomeries are widespread in West Cumberland and in Furness (C). In the 16th century the Company of Mines Royal began extracting copper and lead in both northern and southern Lakeland, and water-powered mills were built and worked wherever the water supply was suitable. Fulling mills were operating in and around Grasmere (C) in the 13th century, using water-powered trip-hammers to replace the slow and tedious process of walking on woollen cloth in a trough of fuller's earth to cleanse and thicken the fabric.

None of these activities made much impact on the countryside. They were small-scale and dispersed. Even the 18th-century blast-furnaces like **Duddon** (100,C) and the bobbin mills of southern Lakeland (105,C) would be barely visible, hidden away in the woods that supplied their raw materials. Large-scale industry, whose imprint was unavoidable, and eventually overpowering, depended on the exploitation of the two major coalfields in the area, the 'Great Northern Coalfield' of County Durham and Northumberland, and the smaller coalfield of West Cumberland.

Three landowning families led the way in West Cumberland, Lowthers in Whitehaven, Senhouses in Maryport, and Curwens in Workington. By 1740 Whitehaven alone was exporting 100,000 tons of coal, mainly to Ireland, and by 1755 the Lowthers had spent half a million pounds on their mines, sinking deep shafts and dealing with the problems of ventilation, flooding, and the lifting of coal from great depths. They built quays at **Whitehaven Harbour** (106,C) to handle outgoing coal and incoming tobacco, and laid out a new town to house an increasing population. Similar development but on a smaller scale took place at Maryport and at Workington.

In County Durham and Northumberland landed families also took the initiative in exploiting local resources, supplying capital for mining and transport, and obtaining excellent returns on their investments. In the 18th century, the 'Grand Allies' – Russells of Brancepeth, Liddells of Ravensworth, and Strathmores of Gibside – opened new mines south of the Tyne and extended the network of wagonways to transport their coal to the river. The **Causey Arch** (98,D) is the most famous relic of the wagonway system, but traces of cuttings, inclines and embankments still remain of long-abandoned routes from the many pits of the area. The Delavals built Seaton Sluice (see 94,N) between 1761 and 1764 to export their coal and other products, and sixty years later, but with the same purpose, Lord Londonderry created Seaham Harbour (D) to export coal from his pits inland.

Huge quantities of coal and its export led to other industries; to shipbuilding on the Tyne and the Wear, to coke production and iron and steel working, to chemical works, glassworks, potteries, and a multitude of ancillary trades. Hand in hand went the development of transport, first as a means of moving coal and other goods, then to meet the needs of passengers. The story of George Stephenson and the development of the locomotive is well known. His birthplace at Wylam-on-Tyne has been preserved (109,N) and is open to visitors, but more evocative still of the early railway age is **North Road Station**, Darlington (99,D) where Stephenson's *Locomotion* is on display as well as other rolling stock of the Stockton and Darlington Railway. The Company's works at Shildon (D) also survive in part, together with the house of the engineer in charge, Timothy Hackworth.

Blackhall Colliery, County Durham.
J ALLAN CASH

The Royal Border Bridge, Berwick-upon-Tweed. AFK

Railways brought a new impetus to the two coalfields and their industries. They revolutionised transport and communication and their engineers created monumental works, viaducts such as those on the Settle to Carlisle railway, and bridges across the great rivers. The Tyne was spanned by the **High Level Bridge** at Newcastle (103,T) and the Tweed by the Royal Border Bridge at Berwick (N), the last link in the east coast route from London to Scotland. Both are the work of Robert Stephenson and in a speech he made in 1850 he catches the spirit of this heroic age:

It seems to me as but yesterday that I was engaged as an assistant in laying out the Stockton and Darlington Railway. Since then the Liverpool and Manchester and a hundred other great works have sprung into existence. As I look back upon these stupendous undertakings, accomplished in so short a time, it seems to me as if we have realised in our generation the fabled powers of the magician's wand. Hills have been cut down and valleys filled up; and when these simple expedients have not sufficed high and magnificent viaducts have been raised and, if mountains stood in the way, tunnels of unexampled magnitude have pierced them through, bearing their triumphant attestation to the indomitable energy of the nation and the unrivalled skill of our artisans.

(Samuel Smiles: *Lives of George and Robert Stephenson*, 1874.)

It is almost incredible how quickly the heavy industries, once dominant, have disappeared. A few mines are still working on the Durham coast, but inland, and in West Cumberland, all the pits have closed, leaving the colliery buildings at the **Beamish Museum** (97,D) the most accessible evidence of the recent past. Iron and steel making have ceased and ship-building has been decimated. Lead-mining (102,D) once widespread through the northern dales is finished. From being the livelihoods of thousands their relics are now the stuff of museums and the study of archaeologists.

97

Beamish North of England Open-Air Museum, County Durham
18th century and later

OS 88 NZ 215540. Beamish. 7 miles (11.2km) SW of Newcastle on A693 between Stanley and Chester-le-Street

[A]

Daniel Defoe, travelling along the road from Durham to Newcastle in the early years of the 18th century (*Tour through the Whole Island of Great Britain*, 1724–7), described how it 'gives a view of the inexhausted store of coal and coal pits, from whence not London only but all the south part of England is continually supplied.' The scene today is very different. There are now few mines still working in the 'Great North Coalfield'.

To preserve the remains of a once great industry, a number of buildings together with their machinery have been assembled at the Beamish Museum from different parts of County Durham. An engine-house, winding-engine, headstock and winding-gear come from Beamish Colliery No. 2 Pit, a few miles distant. The winding-engine, a vertical steam-engine typical of many used in this coalfield, was made by J and G Joicey of Newcastle in 1855. Typical too, are the tall, slender proportions of the engine-house, dictated by the vertical working of the engine.

The coal sorting screens are from Ravensworth Park Drift, Gateshead, and the small powder-house is from Houghton Colliery, near Sunderland. The terrace of six miners' cottages come from Francis Street, Hetton-le-Hole (T), originally built between 1860 and 1865 by the Hetton Coal Company. One is furnished as a colliery office, the others have a vivid sequence of period interiors with furniture from the 1890s onwards. Returning to the colliery, there is no shaft under the winding-gear. To experience conditions underground there are guided tours of Mahogany Drift, near the colliery buildings. This drift-mine was opened in the 1850s and was working until 1958.

Beamish Open Air Museum was opened in 1970. On its 200 acres (80.93ha) there are, in addition to the colliery and drift mine, a re-created town street with an 1860s pub, a number of shops, including a fully-stocked 1920s Co-operative Store, and a working tramway. Also a railway, a transport museum, and a farm. The aim of the museum is to bring to life the social history of the region. It is exceptionally interesting.

98

Causey Arch, County Durham
18th century

OS 88 NZ 201559. Tanfield. On N side of A6076 between Stanley and Gateshead

[A]

Wagonways with wooden rails were used from the beginning of the 17th century for the haulage of coal from mines to the nearest navigable waterway, either river or canal. This was especially so in the North-East where this type of wagonway became known as a 'Newcastle Road' and attracted sightseers from abroad.

Cuttings and embankments were needed to ensure reasonable gradients and bridges to span the deeper channels. Causey Arch is the most famous of these. Indeed it is the world's oldest surviving wagonway bridge. It is a single-span stone bridge crossing Tanfield Beck, and it was built in the 1720s for a wagonway from collieries at Tanfield, linking up with older wagonways going north to the River Tyne. It is 105ft (32 m) wide, 80ft (24 m) high and measures 22ft (6.7 m) across the trackway. It carried two wooden tracks which were used by horse-drawn coal wagons or 'chaldrons'.

Apparently a bridge of lighter construction was in position before 1723, but, inadequate for the loads it was intended to carry, it was replaced by the present bridge in 1727. On a sundial built into one of the piers is the inscription recording the name of its builder, Ralph Woods, a local mason: 'Ra. Wood Mason 1727'.

Mahogany Drift. NORTH OF ENGLAND OPEN AIR MUSEUM, BEAMISH

Causey Arch by Joseph Atkinson, 1804. SCIENCE MUSEUM LONDON

Stephenson's *Locomotion*. N E STEAD

99

Darlington North Road Station, County Durham
19th century

OS 93 NZ 289158. Darlington. In northern part of town by minor road on W side of A167. British Rail signs

[A]

North Road station and its exhibits commemorate the Stockton and Darlington Railway, the first public railway in the world. It was opened on 27 September 1825, amid local celebrations, when a train of 90 tons was drawn by *Locomotion* from Shildon to Stockton at speeds of around 12 to 15 mph. The main purpose of the railway was to transport coal and the first passenger services were provided in horse-drawn coaches. Passenger trains hauled by steam locomotives were introduced in 1833. George Stephenson, the pioneer railway engineer, was responsible both for laying the track and providing locomotives, assisted by his son Robert.

To begin with there were no stations. Tickets were sold at local inns in the same way as for stage-coach journeys. North Road Station was built in 1842 with its main building resembling a Georgian country house. The station platforms and tracks survive under a wooden roof and with modern enclosing walls, and here are displayed *Locomotion* designed by George Stephenson and built at Newcastle, *Derwent* built in 1845 at Darlington, and other historic locomotives. Also a passenger coach of the Stockton and Darlington Railway Company of about 1846. The Company's locomotive Works were at Shildon (D) where Timothy Hackworth was engineer. His house remains, now a small museum, as well as part of the Soho works which he established. A replica of the locomotive *Sans Pareil* is on display. More information about the Stockton and Darlington Railway is provided at the Green Dragon Heritage Centre, Stockton on Tees (Cleveland). The Settle and Carlisle, Ravenglass and Eskdale, and Lakeland and Haverthwaite railways are working railways with historic rolling stock, and routes through magnificent countryside.

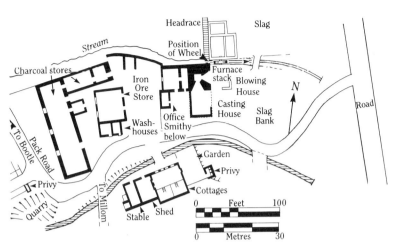

Duddon iron furnace (after Lake District National Park Authority). EH

Duddon iron furnace. RONALD MITCHELL

100

Duddon Iron Furnace, Cumbria
18th century

OS 96 SD 196884. Duddon Bridge. 1 mile (1.6km) W of Broughton in Furness by minor road from Duddon Bridge

[B]

Iron ore was mined in Furness and in West Cumbria during the Middle Ages and smelted at primitive hearths or 'bloomeries', generally in places where large quantities of charcoal were readily available. In the 18th century blast-furnaces revolutionised the smelting process and concentrated iron production on fewer, permanent sites. Large furnace stacks were built consuming greatly increased amounts of ore and fuel, and water power was harnessed to drive bellows pumping air into the combustion chamber.

Duddon is the most complete surviving example in England of an iron producing site with a charcoal-fired blast-furnace, and with the ancillary buildings needed for iron production on a large scale. The furnace stack, 29ft (8.8 m) high, and built of local stone, was charged from above and tapped at its base, with the blowing-house containing the water-powered bellows attached to one side. The water-wheel is missing but one wheel pit has been excavated, and the course of the leat has been traced, bringing water from the river half a mile (0.8km) upstream.

After closure the site became derelict and overgrown. It has been excavated and partially restored, and is now in the care of the Lake District National Park. A permit to visit and a leaflet can be obtained from the Park's Kendal office, Busher Walk, Kendal, Cumbria, LA9 4RH.

101

Honister Slate Quarry, Cumbria
17th century and later

OS 90 NY 215143. Borrowdale. On B5289 Honister Pass at the head of Borrowdale

[D]

Quarrying is one of the staple industries of the northern counties whether for walling stone, roofing materials,

monumental work, lime production, or road metalling. Honister quarry is mentioned in 1753 but is thought to have been worked since at least the mid-17th century. The slate is found high up in Honister Crag, Yew Crag and Rigg Head, at the head of the Honister Pass, and for many years was brought down to the riving and dressing-sheds on sledges steered by a quarryman on foot in front. Later, cableways were made. The inclines and grooves in the rocks worn by cables can still be seen. Until roads improved, slate was taken from the quarry by packhorse over the western edge of Great Gable and Wasdale, by a route known traditionally as 'Mose's Trod', for loading on to boats at Ravenglass.

Honister slate is a distinctive green slate, but Lakeland slate comes in many different shades and colours, as can be seen from even a casual study of local walls and roofs. It is a strong and durable material, excellent for roofs and also for floors and walls. Slate was being

exported through Piel Harbour in 1688 and, before the opening of the Furness railway in 1846, was taken by boat from the sands and creeks of the southern estuaries. In the late 17th century it was used by Sir Christopher Wren at the Royal Hospital, Chelsea, and at Kensington Palace. It is still being exported widely, but not from Honister which is now closed.

No mention of quarries, however brief, would be complete without reference to the Shap granite quarries (C). Opened in 1864 with the coming of the Lancaster to Carlisle railway, the vivid, mottled, 'pink' granite is to be seen on Victorian buildings, notably the Albert Memorial, and in many churchyards. A second quarry produces blue granite chippings for railway ballast. Visits to active quarries are not advisable unless by special invitation.

102

Killhope Crushing Mill, County Durham
19th century

OS 87 NY 826430. St John's Chapel. 5 miles (8km) NW of St John's Chapel on A689 to Alston

[A]

Lead ore was mined extensively in the northern dales and evidence of disused workings is abundant. After mining, the ore had to be treated to separate the lead from other minerals and to make it ready for smelting. Often it was broken up by hand, using small flat-headed hammer-like tools called 'buckers', and frequently the work was done by women. However, at Killhope the ore was extremely hard and crushing had to be done by iron rollers driven by a water-powered wheel.

The wheel is the most spectacular part of the workings. It is 33ft 8in (approx. 10 m) in diameter, made of iron, and dates from about 1860. It is over-shot, that is to say, it was turned by water brought in a high trough to its upper part, and it powered four sets of crushing rollers. After crushing, the fragments of ore were washed in

Honister slate quarry. VISIONBANK/ROB TALBOT

Killhope crushing mill. P NIXON/DURHAM COUNTY COUNCIL ENVIRONMENT DEPARTMENT

running water to separate the heavier galena (lead sulphide) from the rest.

An exhibition in the visitor centre provides an introduction to the site. The tour of site begins at the smithy which had above it a lodging for miners and other workmen who boarded here during the week. Part of the lodging has been restored with appropriate furniture. Near this building is the entrance to Park Level Mine with rails going from the mine to the 'bousesteads', storage areas for the ore before treatment. In the valley bottom are settling troughs for washing the ore and beyond these is an earth ramp, continued originally by a wooden bridge, which took trucks of ore to the crushing rollers next to the wheel.

The mill was closed at the beginning of the century and stood derelict until 1966. Since then clearance and excavation have recovered much of the workings, and parts are being restored. The site is owned and managed by the Durham County Council and is open to visitors.

Treated ore from Killhope was taken to Nenthead (C) 3 miles (4.5km) to the west, where the remains of a lead smelter and associated buildings survive. Killhope ore was also taken to Allendale (N) 8 miles (12.5km) to the north where isolated chimneys on the hillsides mark the end of underground flues, several miles long, taking furnace gases from the smelters in the valley.

103

Newcastle upon Tyne High Level Bridge, Tyne and Wear
19th century

OS 88 NZ 252637. Newcastle upon Tyne

[D]

The High Level Bridge is a great feat of engineering, somewhat dwarfed now by nearby structures, but when first built, huge and dominating. It was the key to railway expansion north and south of the river. Early bridges across the Tyne were at river level with roads climbing the steep banks on either side. A rail-crossing had to bridge the valley and, to achieve this, two railway companies, the Newcastle and Berwick and the Newcastle and Darlington, jointly provided the finance. Robert Stephenson was appointed consulting engineer in association with Thomas Harrison, resident engineer of the Company. Work began in 1846 and the bridge was opened by Queen Victoria on 28 September 1849.

The bridge has six arches made of iron, with spans of 125ft (38.1 m), supported by five pairs of stone piers, the tallest being 146ft (44.5 m) high. These are underpinned in the river bed by timber piles driven in to a depth of 32ft (9.7 m), using James Nasmyth's newly invented steam-hammer. There are two decks. The upper deck, supported on columns above the arches, carries the three railway tracks. The lower deck, suspended from the arches, has a 20ft (6.1 m) roadway and flanking footpaths. Tolls on road users and pedestrians were levied until 1937.

A natural companion to the High Level bridge is Newcastle Central Station opened in 1850 and designed by John Dobson. The portico is by Thomas Prosser. Also in Newcastle is Dean Street Bridge, built in 1849.

The railway station at Monkwearmouth in the northern part of Sunderland and close to Monkwearmouth's historic church (29,T), is an outstanding example of early railway architecture. It was designed by John Dobson in 1848 in neo-classical style and has a giant Ionic portico in front of its main building. Closed to traffic, it is now used as a transport museum.

High Level Bridge, Newcastle upon Tyne. J ALLAN CASH

Ryhope pumping station. THE SUNDERLAND ECHO

104

Ryhope Pumping Station, Tyne and Wear
19th century

OS 88 NZ 404524. Sunderland.
3 miles (4.8km) S of Sunderland at
Ryhope on A1018 and minor road.
Signed 'Engines Museum'

[B]

Heavy engineering is synonymous with
the workshops and shipyards clustered
on the banks of the rivers Tyne and
Wear. The Newcastle firm of R and W
Hawthorn supplied the two engines at
Ryhope, 100 hp double-acting rotative
beam-engines, which began work in
1869 and ceased operation in 1967.

The pumping station was built by the
Sunderland and South Shields Water
Company, on land acquired in 1865, to
meet an increasing demand for water,
which at Ryhope was pumped from a
depth of 250ft (76 m) at a rate of 3
million gallons a day. It was pumped to a
reservoir in the grounds which supplied
both Sunderland and South Shields.
Eventually seepage of salt into the wells,
and cheaper supplies from elsewhere,
forced the closure of the pumping
station. The south engine, the last in
use, was stopped on 1 July 1967. Steam
was raised originally in six Cornish
boilers, but these were replaced in 1908
by three larger Lancashire boilers.

The beam-engines are magnificent
examples of Victorian engineering,
impressive in size and extremely
reliable, giving nearly 100 years of

continuous service. Worth noting too
are the buildings. The engine-house
with its Dutch gables, domestic
windows, and roof lantern has more the
character of a small town hall than a
water-works, though the tall chimney
suggests its true function. The pumping
station is now run by a local Trust which
arranges access. The former coal store is
used for exhibitions.

Some way away but of interest to
pumping engine enthusiasts is the Tees
Cottage Pumping Station, Coniscliffe
Road, Darlington (D). It was built in the
1840s and has a 1904 compound beam
engine. It can be found 2 miles (3km)
from the centre of Darlington on the
A67 Barnard Castle road.

105

Stott Park Bobbin Mill, Cumbria
19th century

OS 97 SD 373883. Finsthwaite.
1 mile (1.6km) N of Newby Bridge at
S end of Windermere, by minor road
to Finsthwaite

[A] EH

Bobbin making was a thriving industry
in Cumbria in the 19th century,
stimulated by the huge demand for
cotton bobbins from Lancashire mills.
The raw material, mainly birch, was
obtained from local woods, and water for
driving the lathes was abundant. At first,
existing water-powered mills were
converted to bobbin-making. Later they
were purpose built. Stott Park Mill was
built in 1835 by John Harrison, a local
landowner, and started production in

Stott Park bobbin mill. EH

1836. Originally it consisted of a two-storeyed building with a water-wheel at one end and, probably, a small coppice shed. Water came from the mill-pond fed by a tarn three quarters of a mile (1km) away. Later, a second lathe-shop was added, also a boiler-house with a drying-room over and a larger coppice shed. The water-wheel does not survive. It was replaced by turbines, supplemented later by a steam-engine. Finally, in 1941, electric motors were installed.

In the middle of the 19th century forty-nine bobbin mills were at work in southern Lakeland, but, with a decline in the cotton industry and foreign competition, many mills went out of business towards the end of the century. Stott Park turned to other products such as handle-making, to supplement bobbin manufacture, but the increasing use of plastic for bobbins and handles finally forced its closure in 1971. It escaped demolition and today is a unique example of a Victorian bobbin mill, fully equipped and virtually unaltered. There are occasional working demonstrations of tools and machinery. The Museum of Lakeland Life and Industry in Kendal (68,C) has a small section devoted to bobbin making, among its many other exhibits.

106

Whitehaven Harbour, Cumbria
17th century and later

OS 89 NZ 973183. Whitehaven. 39 miles (63km) SW of Carlisle on A595 [C]

Until the 17th century Whitehaven, Workington, and Maryport were fishing villages on the Cumbrian coast. All three were transformed by the coal trade promoted by local land-owning families, the Curwens at Workington, the Senhouses at Maryport, and the Lowthers at Whitehaven.

At Whitehaven the first quay was built by Christopher Lowther in 1634. It was lengthened in 1665 and 1687 and is one of the oldest remaining coal wharves

Whitehaven harbour. R BEWLEY

in Britain, although now put to other uses. A second quay was built in 1741; West Quay was constructed between 1824 and 1839, and Queen's Harbour was completed in 1876. In the 18th century Whitehaven was the third most important port in England, exporting coal, especially to Dublin, and importing tobacco, sugar, rum, and other goods from the West Indies. Of particular interest in the harbour is the lighthouse on the Old Quay. It dates from about 1710. Originally it had an oil lantern but a gas light was installed in 1834.

Parallel with the development of the harbour, the Lowthers created the first planned town in England since the Middle Ages. It was laid out on a grid pattern with St Nicholas's church at the centre. An Assembly Room was built (Howgill Street), a mansion for the Lowthers (rebuilt later and now part of the hospital), and houses of different degrees of quality. Some of the 18th-century houses survive among later rebuilding, and a walk through the streets is both an exercise in detection and an agreeable experience now that skilful conservation has rescued streets and buildings once sunk in decay. St Nicholas's church was rebuilt in 1883. St James's church, built in 1752–3, is more rewarding. It has a fine Georgian interior.

Little remains of the once flourishing coal and iron industries of this area. Candlestick Chimney is the only surviving part of a colliery engine house built in 1850, and nearby is Duke Pit fan-casing which once housed a 36ft diameter wooden ventilation fan. Elsewhere, abandoned workings and former pit villages are the most prominent reminders of the West Cumberland coalfield which was the foundation of Whitehaven's earlier prosperity.

Lighthouse, Whitehaven. RCHME

10

Birthplaces, Literary Shrines, Monuments and Follies

In 1801, at the age of seventy-eight, William Hutton of Birmingham walked to Northumberland, tramped along Hadrian's Wall from end to end, and returned home, on foot, covering in all some 600 miles. He recorded his observations and experiences in *The History of the Roman Wall*, published a year after his pilgrimage. Hutton was drawn to Hadrian's Wall by a love of history and antiquities, but others were journeying to the North of England in search of the Picturesque. They were looking for untamed landscapes, for scenery that was wild and awe-inspiring, and in the Lake District especially, they found what they desired. They were helped in their search by guidebooks which described 'stations' from which the best views could be obtained, and which gave practical help with mileages between towns, and lists of inns for overnight stays. By the end of the 18th century visitors to the Lake District were travelling on well established tourist routes, knowing what they wished to see and staying in places that catered for their needs.

The number of visitors was still comparatively small and mainly limited to the well-to-do. On Ullswater they could take to the water on barges fitted with brass cannons whose explosions made the mountains echo wonderfully, and at Conishead Priory a hermitage could be inspected, with a 'hermit' in attendance. Another hermitage, on Mr Wilkinson's estate at Yanwath, was roofed with thatch and lined with moss, but without a paid retainer to provide the human interest. Such delights were not designed for the huge influx of people brought by the railways, an intrusion resisted by Wordsworth who objected vigorously to the building of the line from Kendal to Windermere in 1847. Ironically, many were attracted by his own writings, and especially his *Guide to the Lakes*, first published in 1810 and frequently re-issued.

Nowadays Wordsworth and his poetry attract visitors in ever larger numbers, to his birthplace in **Cockermouth** (116,C), to the school at Hawkshead (C), to **Dove Cottage** (108,C) in Grasmere, and to **Rydal Mount** (113,C), his last home. Ruskin's house at **Brantwood** (107,C) on Coniston Water is another place of literary pilgrimage, and so too is **Hill Top Farm** (111,C) at Near Sawrey, purchased by Beatrix Potter in 1905 and lived in intermittently until her marriage in 1913.

Wordsworth's birthplace in Cockermouth is a fine Georgian house, befitting the steward of the powerful Lowther family. Thomas Bewick's birthplace at **Cherryburn** (114,N) in the valley of the Tyne was a modest farmhouse lived in by a family of ten, Thomas being the eldest of eight children. His genius was expressed in wood engraving. George Stephenson's beginnings were humbler still. His birthplace is at **Wylam** (109,N), also on the River Tyne but a few miles further east. Accommodation for the Stephensons was a single room for a family of eight, but from these beginnings came a man whose achievements transformed the industrial life of Britain.

The number of picturesque monuments and follies in the northern counties is small. For the most part nature needed little embellishment, and large estates, the usual home of architectural follies, were not as dominant as elsewhere. Nevertheless there are some splendid pieces. The Greek temple commemorating John George Lambton, at Penshaw (112,T), is wonderfully dramatic, as black as pitch and superbly positioned on a Durham hill, dominating the surrounding countryside. Equally commanding, but in an urban setting, is the Grey Monument in Newcastle, a huge Doric column with the figure of Earl Grey, author of the 1832 Reform Act, perched

Brizlee Tower, Alnwick. AFK

on top.

Alnwick (47,N) has the largest number of picturesque remains. Two are genuinely medieval. The gatehouse of Alnwick Abbey is within the grounds, and so too are the eloquent ruins of Hulne Priory in which a gothick summer-house was built by the 1st duke of Northumberland. Entirely 18th-century at Alnwick are Brizlee Tower and Ratcheugh Observatory, the first a tall, circular prospect tower with gothick trimmings, and the second a sham castle on a cliff.

At Wallington (96,N) Sir Walter Blackett built a mock fort, 'Codjah's Crag', and elsewhere in Northumberland there are castellated kennels (Nunwick) and a castellated village school (Hartburn). At Bishop Auckland (32) in County Durham, Bishop Trevor built a deer fold in the episcopal park with a battlemented enclosure and 'fortified' tower, and at Netherby in Cumbria a sham castle hides the estate's salmon coops behind gothick towers equipped with arrow slits. Also in Cumbria are the decorated farms of the 11th duke of Norfolk at **Greystoke** (110,C), perhaps the most entertaining of these light-hearted constructions. For those who wish to pursue these intriguing oddities in more detail and further afield, Barbara Jones's *Follies and Grottoes* (Constable, 2nd edn, 1974) is an excellent guide, with county lists.

107

Brantwood, Cumbria
19th century

OS 97 SD 312958. Coniston. On minor road on E side of Coniston Water, 2 miles (3.2km) SE of Coniston

[A]

John Ruskin bought Brantwood in 1871 and moved into it the following year. It was little more than a large cottage at the time of purchase. Ruskin described it disparagingly as 'a mere shed of rotten timber and loose stones', but it enjoyed, as he well knew, one of the finest views

in the Lake District. He lived here until his death in 1900, aged eighty.

Ruskin was the greatest art critic and one of the most original thinkers of the 19th century. He championed the work of J M W Turner, supported the Pre-Raphaelites, and was a powerful influence on William Morris. His interests embraced art and architecture, geology, natural history, and social reform. He taught at the newly formed Working Men's College in London, was Slade Professor of Art at Oxford, and founded the Guild of St George, a forlorn attempt to create model communities of cottagers and cottage industries.

His principal books were published before moving to Brantwood but he continued to write and in 1889 completed his autobiography, *Praeterita*. He extended the house, adding a bedroom turret for better views of the lake, a new dining-room, studio,

stables, coach-house, and servants' quarters, and increased the original 16 acres (6.47ha) of grounds into a substantial estate. He filled the house with a magnificent collection of paintings, books, and manuscripts, acquired during his lifetime, including many works by Turner. Much of Ruskin's collection was sold in the 1930s, but some of his furniture and part of his library remain, together with paintings by Ruskin and his contemporaries.

In Coniston village is the Ruskin Museum which is part of the Coniston Mechanics Institute and Literary Society. Ruskin's grave is in Coniston churchyard. The Victorian steam yacht *Gondola*, in service on Coniston Water between 1859 and 1940, has been restored by the National Trust and sails regularly from Coniston pier to other parts of the lakeside, including Brantwood.

Brantwood. CL

Dove Cottage, Grasmere. EDWIN SMITH

108

Dove Cottage, Cumbria
17th–18th century and later

OS 90 NY 343069. Grasmere.
3 miles (4.8km) NW of Ambleside
on A591 at Town End

[A]

William Wordsworth and his sister
Dorothy moved into Dove Cottage in
December 1799. It had been an inn, the
Dove and Olive Branch, but in
Wordsworth's time it was known simply
as 'Town End', the general name of this
small hamlet. Wordsworth first saw the
cottage during 1799 while on a walking
tour with his friend and fellow poet,
Samuel Taylor Coleridge. He wrote to
his sister with the news of 'a small house
at Grasmere empty, which, perhaps, we
may take', and they were in the house in
time to celebrate her birthday on
Christmas Day 1799. She was twenty-
eight. Wordsworth was twenty-nine.

Their stay at Dove Cottage was a
happy one. Wordsworth wrote some of
his finest poetry here. Dorothy saw to

domestic matters, accompanied him on
his walks, and compiled a journal in
which she recorded, from 1800 to 1803,
the details of their daily life. They visited
Coleridge, walking the mountain passes
to reach Keswick where he was now
living; they planted the garden behind
their cottage; and they absorbed the
beauty and the grandeur of the
surrounding mountains.

In 1802 William married Mary
Hutchinson, a childhood friend from
Penrith, and brought her to the cottage
where, together with Dorothy, all three
lived until 1808. Here too were born
three of Wordsworth's children, John,
Dora, and Thomas.

'Cottage' is rather misleading.
Although small, it is a genteel property,
not a peasant dwelling. It is stone-built,
of two storeys, with a roof of Lakeland
slate. On the ground floor are two rooms
and a kitchen, and a small larder which
has a running stream under its stone-
paved floor. On the upper floor are four
small rooms, one of them an upstairs
sitting room. It has many items
associated with the Wordsworths, and
although it attracts visitors by the

thousand its atmosphere is surprisingly
intimate and evocative.

In 1808 the Wordsworths moved to
Allan Bank in Grasmere. Dove Cottage
was let to Thomas de Quincey who kept
it until 1830, followed by a variety of
tenants until 1890 when a trust was
established for its preservation. The
Wordsworth Trust still manages the
property and provides an excellent
exhibition in a building nearby.

William and Mary Wordsworth, their
daughter Dora, his sister Dorothy, and
other members of the family are buried
in St Oswald's churchyard, Grasmere.

109

George Stephenson's
Birthplace, Northumberland
18th century

OS 88 NZ 126650. 8 miles (12.8km)
W of Newcastle on A69 and minor
road. The cottage is E of Wylam
village, half a mile's walk from the
War Memorial car park

[A] NT

George Stephenson was born at Wylam
on the north bank of the River Tyne on
9 July 1781. He was the second of the
six children of Robert and Mabel
Stephenson. His father worked at that
time at Wylam Colliery and their rented
accommodation was in a cottage, known
as 'Street House'. It stood beside a
wooden wagonway taking horse-drawn
chaldrons of coal from the local pits to
riverside staithes.

At fourteen George Stephenson
became assistant fireman to his father at
Dewley Colliery and was employed at
various collieries in the area before
becoming, in 1812, engine-wright at
Killingworth Colliery, north-east of
Newcastle. Here he interested the
Colliery owners in steam locomotives
and with their support built a
locomotive to his own design in the
engine-shop at West Moor. In 1819 he
laid a railway at Hetton colliery and in
1821 was appointed engineer to the
Stockton and Darlington Railway
Company, newly established to provide
transport from inland pits to coal
wharves at Stockton-on-Tees

(Cleveland). The story of this railway is told elsewhere (99,D). In 1829 Stephenson was appointed engineer to the Liverpool and Manchester Railway and won the famous trial at Rainhill with his locomotive *Rocket*. He became chief engineer to various other companies and until 1845 was involved with railway schemes throughout the country. He died in 1848 and is buried at Trinity Church, Chesterfield, near his last home.

Stephenson's name is synonymous with railways. He also invented a miner's safety lamp different from, but contemporary with, the better known lamp of Sir Humphry Davy. He was a man of great physical strength and powers of endurance, and an engineer of genius. In his lifetime he revolutionised transport and transformed the face of England. He accepted, and was pleased with, professional recognition but refused all political honours in England including an invitation to stand for Parliament. His birthplace is part of a cottage built about 1750. The Stephenson family lived here in one room until 1789. It is now in the care of the National Trust and the single room, furnished as in the Stephensons' time, is open to visitors.

110

Greystoke Farms, Cumbria
18th century

OS 90 NY 459309, NY 453309 and NY 463314. Greystoke. On B5288 and minor road between Penrith and Greystoke village

[D]

The Honourable Charles Howard, son of the 10th duke of Norfolk, was born at Greystoke Castle in 1746. In 1780 he was elected Member of Parliament for Carlisle and held the seat until 1786, when he succeeded his father as the 11th duke. His political views were radical. He actively opposed the government's policy towards the American colonists, and offended George III by proposing a toast at a political dinner to 'Our Sovereign's health – the majesty of the people'.

He was, like other members of the Howard family, fond of architectural conceits, and on his Cumbrian estate he built, probably about 1789, three extraordinary farms. Two, Bunker's Hill and Fort Putnam, were given mock fortifications and the third, Spire House,

Spire House, Greystoke. CL

a tower and lead-covered steeple. Bunker's Hill is named after an American victory in their war against the British, and Fort Putnam after one of the American generals, no doubt to the intense irritation of the duke's Tory neighbours. All three are working farms but their fanciful architectural trimmings may be seen from nearby roads. Nearer Penrith, at NY 493298, is Greystoke Pillar, a tall obelisk on a square plinth.

111

Hill Top Farm, Cumbria
17th century

OS 97 SD 370955. Near Sawrey. On B5285 2 miles (3.2km) SE of Hawkshead, or by ferry from Bowness and B5285

[A] NT

Beatrix Potter purchased Hill Top farm in 1905. She continued to live with her parents in London for most of the year, but slipped away whenever she could to this modest house which gave her the freedom to write and paint, and was the background for Jemima Puddleduck, Tom Kitten and her other extraordinary creatures. The farmhouse dates from the 17th century and has the rough-cast walls and slated roof characteristic of this area. The sash windows are later insertions, but no changes have been made in recent years. It has remained as it was in Beatrix Potter's lifetime, with her furniture and personal possessions still in place.

In 1913 Beatrix Potter married William Heelis and moved into Castle

George Stephenson's birthplace, Wylam. NT/DEREK WIDDICOMBE

Cottage, a larger house bought four years earlier. She took up farming and acquired over the years a considerable amount of land and other property in the area. In her youth she had met Canon Rawnsley, a champion of conservation and co-founder of the National Trust, and during her lifetime she made generous contributions to the Trust, often anonymously. On her death in 1943 much of her property passed to the Trust by bequest, including Hill Top Farm which she had kept for thirty years as her personal museum, unoccupied except for a farm manager in one part.

In Hawkshead the Beatrix Potter Gallery (NT), housed in what was once her husband's office, has a number of her original drawings on display, but the town itself, once a thriving market centre, is worth visiting in its own right. Wordsworthians will wish to see the Old Grammar School and a little outside the town, at Colthouse, the cottage in which William and his brother boarded while attending the school.

112

Lord Durham's Monument, Tyne and Wear
19th century

OS 88 NZ 334544. Penshaw. 4 miles (6.4km) SW of Sunderland on A183, or from A1(M)

[A] NT

Two champions of parliamentary reform are commemorated by monuments of some splendour. Charles Grey was born at Falloden near Alnwick in 1764. He was Member of Parliament for Northumberland from 1786 to 1807, when he succeeded his father as the 2nd Earl Grey, and in 1830 became Prime Minister. During his government the great Reform Act of 1832 became law, and in his honour a giant column crowned with his statue stands in the centre of Newcastle at the head of Grey Street.

Lord Durham's monument, Penshaw. AFK

His fellow reformer was John George Lambton, Member of Parliament for County Durham from 1813 to 1828. He was created 1st earl of Durham in 1828, became a member of Grey's Government and took a leading role in the preparation of the first Reform Bill. In 1834 he was appointed ambassador to St Petersburg, and in 1838 was sent to Canada as High Commissioner to resolve political differences. The 'Durham Report' became the cornerstone of the future government of that country. His monument in Britain stands on the crest of a hill near the village of Penshaw. It was built in 1844, four years after his death, and is a copy of the Temple of Theseus in Athens. Smoke-blackened and austere, it has until recently commanded a landscape of collieries and slagheaps, now becoming clearer and greener with pit closures and reclamation. It is visible for miles around, 'an apparition of the Acropolis under hyperborean skies.' Pevsner, *Buildings of England, County Durham*.

113

Rydal Mount, Cumbria
16th–19th centuries

OS 90 NY 364064. Rydal. Between Grasmere and Ambleside off A591

[A]

The Wordsworths moved from the Parsonage in Grasmere to Rydal Mount in May 1813. The house stands on a

Hilltop Farm, Near Sawrey. NT

Rydal Mount. J ALLAN CASH

wooded hillside above St Mary's church, Rydal, between Grasmere and Ambleside. It was built in the 16th century as a farmhouse, known as 'Keenes', but in the 18th century the house was extended and improved by the then owners, the Knott family, and re-named 'Rydal Mount' in the early years of the 19th century. Wordsworth added a study on the top floor, and laid out the gardens which are still largely as he designed them.

Rydal Mount was Wordsworth's home until his death in 1850. He lived here with his wife Mary, their surviving children Dora, John and William, his sister Dorothy, and his wife's sister, Sara Hutchinson. His income improved substantially in 1813, when he was appointed 'Distributor of Stamps' for the county of Westmorland, and at Rydal Mount the Wordsworths entertained more freely and received a large number of visitors. However, William himself was little changed. He continued to walk and to write, and while at Rydal completed nearly half his poems. In 1843 he was appointed Poet Laureate.

The house contains furniture used by the Wordsworth family, portraits, personal belongings, and a collection of first editions of his work. Near the house

is the field purchased by Wordsworth in 1825 when their continued tenancy of Rydal Mount was in doubt. It was bought with the intention of building a new home, but, when this was not required, Wordsworth gave the field to his daughter, Dora. On her death in 1847 Wordsworth planted it with daffodils in her memory.

Rydal Mount is privately owned, the property of a direct descendant of Wordsworth, and is open to the public. 'Dora's Field' is in the care of the National Trust.

114
Thomas Bewick's Birthplace, Northumberland
18th century

OS 88 NZ 075628. Cherryburn. 9 miles (14.5km) W of Newcastle on A695 and minor road from Mickley Square

[A] NT

Thomas Bewick was born at Cherryburn, close to the River Tyne, in 1753. He was the eldest of eight children. His father, John Bewick, was a tenant farmer who also leased a small coal-mine at Eltringham nearby. It was not a large business. The mine supplied coal for local people rather than for export, but it supplemented the meagre return from the few acres of farmland, bringing the family a modest income rather than a substantial fortune.

Thomas attended school first in Mickley and then across the river in Ovingham where the school was held in

Thomas Bewick's birthplace, Cherryburn. NT/EDDIE RYLE-HODGES

the vicarage. At the age of fourteen he was apprenticed to Ralph Beilby, an engraver, in Newcastle, and worked for him for seven years, completing his apprenticeship in 1774. He moved back to Cherryburn, then worked briefly in London before returning to Newcastle to join Ralph Beilby as partner in his business. Their premises were in St Nicholas's churchyard in Newcastle.

Bewick was a superb craftsman. He revived the art of wood engraving in England and with new techniques and great artistry captured in miniature, but with extraordinarily fine detail, the birds, animals and scenes of country life. His most famous works are his illustrations in the *General History of Quadrupeds*, published in 1790, and those in the two volume *History of British Birds*, 1797, but his genius illuminates many other books including the delightful illustrations he provided for an edition of *Aesop's Fables* published in 1818.

The small farmhouse he was born in at Cherryburn still survives although at one time it was used as a byre. There is also a larger house built by his descendants. An exhibition of Bewick's work includes the tools and type of printing press used in his day. His grave is in Ovingham churchyard next to that of his wife.

115

Washington Old Hall, Tyne and Wear
Middle Ages and 17th century

OS 88 NZ 312166. Washington. 10 miles (16km) SE of Newcastle on A195

[A] NT

The Old Hall stands near the church in the village of Washington, now surrounded by the buildings and estates of Washington New Town. For five generations it was the home of the ancestors of George Washington, first President of the United States, and it was held by Washingtons and their descendants until 1613. It was then sold and had a succession of owners until, in

Washington Old Hall. NT

later years, it was divided into tenements, fell into disrepair, and was threatened with demolition. It was saved and restored with American support, opened in 1955, and two years later given to the National Trust.

Viewed from the outside the present house looks entirely 17th-century. It is an attractive, gabled building with a symmetrical entrance front, and central doorway leading into the great hall. However, on entering the house it is immediately apparent that parts are medieval. At the kitchen end of the great hall are two medieval doorways and in the kitchen itself is part of a medieval window. The rest is largely 17th-century, although many of the fittings, the staircase, panelling, furniture and some of the fireplaces, have been brought from elsewhere as part of the general restoration. Parts of the upper floor are in use but the ground floor and one of the bedrooms are open to the public.

From County Durham members of the Washington family moved to Warton in Lancashire, and then to Northamptonshire where Lawrence Washington built Sulgrave Manor. His descendant, John Washington, emigrated to America in 1656 and

settled in Virginia. It was his great grandson, George, born in 1732, who was to become commander of the American forces in the War of Independence, and in 1789 the first President of the United States.

116

Wordsworth House, Cumbria
18th century

OS 89 NY 118307. Cockermouth. 26 miles (41.8km) SW of Carlisle on A595

[A] NT

William Wordsworth was born in Cockermouth on 7 April 1770, the second son of John and Ann Wordsworth who had five children, Richard, the eldest, Wiliam, Dorothy, John and Christopher.

The house did not belong to the family. It was built in 1745 by Joshua Lucock, sheriff of Cumberland, and purchased in 1764 by Sir James Lowther, the owner of estates and coal-mines in the area, but whose principal residence was at Lowther (70,C) near Penrith. John Wordsworth, a lawyer, was Sir James's steward, managing his affairs in the locality and having the use of the house as part reimbursement for

William Wordsworth, aged 36, by Henry Edridge, 1806. THE WORDSWORTH TRUST

Wordsworth House, Cockermouth, AFK

his services.

It is an elegant Georgian building with the relaxed air of a country mansion although it is in one of the principal streets of the town and close to the centre. At the back, the grounds run down to the River Derwent ending with a paved walk above the river, the 'Terrace Walk', described in Wordsworth's poem *The Prelude* among recollections of his childhood at Cockermouth.

In 1778 Ann Wordsworth died and the children were sent to stay with relatives. William and his brothers were placed with an aunt and uncle in Penrith and from 1779 William attended the Grammar School at Hawkshead as a boarder, returning occasionally to Cockermouth to visit his father. John Wordsworth stayed in the family house until 1783, but his death in that year ended the Wordsworth connection.

The interior of the house has been altered during a succession of owners, but it retains a number of original features and has furniture associated with the Wordsworths, brought to the house from elsewhere. In 1938 it was threatened with demolition. Money for its purchase was raised by public appeal and subsequently the house was placed in the care of the National Trust.

Dove Cottage (108,C) at Grasmere, and Rydal Mount (113,C), other homes of William and Dorothy Wordsworth in the Lake District, are also open to visitors. Enthusiasts may also visit the Old Grammar School at Hawkshead.

Bibliography

The publications of the Cumberland and Westmorland Antiquarian and Archaeological Society, the Society of Antiquaries of Newcastle, and the Durham and Northumberland Archaeological Society, are invaluable sources for the prehistory and history of the northern counties. So too are the older county histories which are listed in the introductions to Nikolaus Pevsner's *Buildings of England* series mentioned below.

The Royal Commission on the Historical Monuments of England (RCHME) has published an inventory of sites and buildings for the former county of Westmorland, as well as a separate report on sheilings and bastles for a wider area. Guide books and leaflets are often available in churches and country houses, and at those properties of English Heritage which are staffed. More general works which may be found useful are detailed below:

P Allen, *The Old Galleries of Cumbria and the Early Wool Trade*, Abbot Hall, Kendal, 1984.

B Allsopp and R Christie, *Historic Architecture of Northumberland*, Oriel Press, 1969.

F Atkinson, *Industrial Archaeology of North East England*, 2 vols., David & Charles, 1974.

M W Beresford, *Lost Villages of England*, Alan Sutton, 1983.

K J Bonser, *The Drovers*, Macmillan, 1970.

J Collingwood Bruce, *Handbook to the Roman Wall*, 13th edn, revised and extended by C M Daniels, Hill, 1978.

D J Breeze and B Dobson, *Hadrian's Wall*, Penguin, 1987.

R A Brown, *English Castles*, Batsford, 1976.

R W Brunskill, *Traditional Farm Buildings of Britain*, Gollancz, 1987.

D M Butler, *Quaker Meeting Houses of the Lake Counties*, Friends Historical Society, 1978.

L Butler and C Given-Wilson, *Medieval Monasteries of Great Britain*, Michael Joseph, 1979.

T Clare, *Archaeological Sites of the Lake District*, Moorland, 1981.

A Clifton-Taylor, *The Pattern of English Building*, Faber and Faber, 1972.

G Darley, *Villages of Vision*, Architectural Press, 1975.

T Darvill, *Prehistoric Britain*, Batsford, 1987.

H Davies, *A Walk Around the Lakes*, Arrow, 1987.

G W Dolbey, *The Architectural Expression of Methodism*, Epworth Press, 1964.

Celia Fiennes, *Journeys*, ed. C Morris, Macdonald, 1984.

D Fleming, *Exploring Museums, North East England*, HMSO, 1989.

D Hague and R Christie, *Lighthouses, their architecture, history and archaeology*, Gomer Press, 1975.

N Higham, *The Northern Counties to AD 1000*, Longman, 1986.

B P Hindle, *Roads and Trackways of the Lake District*, Moorland, 1984.

T Hopkin, *Northumberland National Park*, Webb & Bower, 1987.

S Johnson, *Hadrian's Wall*, Batsford/English Heritage, 1989.

B Jones, *Follies and Grottoes*, Constable, 1974.

J D Marshal and M Davies-Shiel, *Industrial Archaeology of the Lake Counties*, David & Charles, 1977.

F Newton, *The Northumberland Landscape*, Hodder & Stoughton, 1972.

N Nicolson, *The Lakers*, Robert Hale, 1955.

N Pevsner, *The Buildings of England: County Durham, Cumberland and Westmorland, Northumberland*, Penguin, various dates.

D Phillips, *Exploring Museums, North West England and the Isle of Man*, HMSO, 1989.

H G Ramm, R W McDowall and E Mercer (RCHME), *Shielings and Bastles*, HMSO, 1970.

J M Robinson, *The Architecture of Northern England*, Macmillan, 1986.

W Rollinson, *Life and Tradition in the Lake District*, Dent, 1974.

A Wainwright, *Pictorial Guides to the Lakeland Fells*, Kendal, various dates.

J Wyatt, *Lake District National Park*, Webb & Bower, 1987.

Tawny Owl. Wood engraving by Thomas Bewick, 1797. NT

Index

Maps

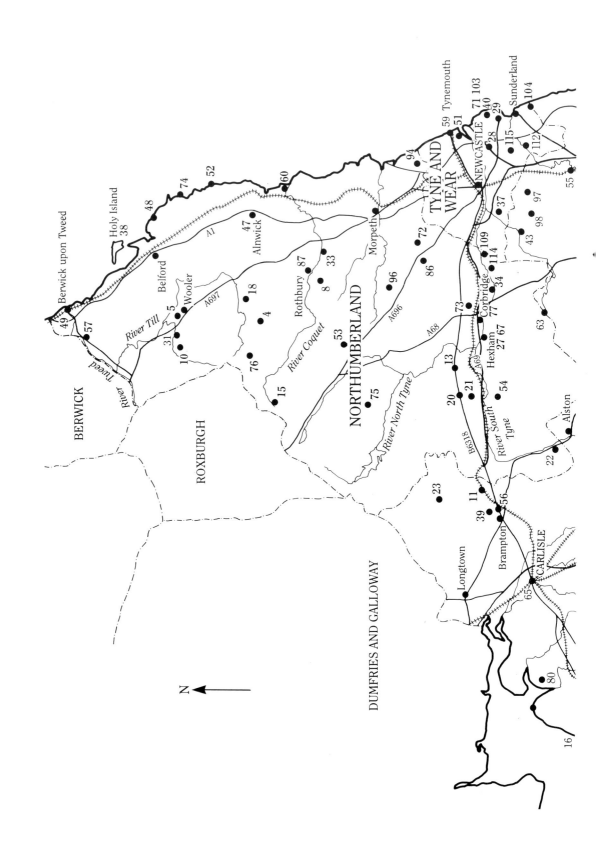